JOURNEYS CLOSE TO HOME

Explorations of an Imagined City

Journeys Close to Home

Explorations of an Imagined City

NICK SMILLIE

www.1889books.co.uk

ISBN: 978-1-915045-46-1

For Mum

In memory of Kate, Ron

and their generation.

We're missing them

Contents

An Imagined City

Following the usual advice, I decided to write about the things close to me. Truth be told, there wasn't much choice at first – this would have to be a travelogue of journeys within walking distance, or else through time from a static point, composed with my eyes closed.

But when I went out in search of the city I call home and believed I knew, I made an unexpected discovery. The cities described by the people I spoke to were entirely unfamiliar – places I'd never visited.

Taxi drivers, factory owners, mechanics, musicians, nail technicians, rock climbers, river anglers, estate agents, members of religious congregations – each possessed their own, unique city map, marked with familiar gennels, roads and nodes of significance. Our maps overlapped only at rare coordinates, generating sparks of recognition which, for a second, bound us together.

But even in those flashes of connection all we really shared were words and superficial impressions. What those places meant to each of us was entirely personal, products of our own tangled associations, to the other, unknowable.

Every one of us believes we live in a real city – a place everyone else can see in the same way. But the only one we know is an unsound construction of the mind, built from fragments of memories, myths and hearsay, fleeting impressions and personal obsessions, familiar ground and incomplete information.

Other people's cities are alien places, subjects in which I can claim no authority. All I can talk about is my imagined city, hoping that someone, somewhere will smile in a satisfying moment of shared understanding – when our paths cross at a familiar intersection.

Start Here

But where's the best place to start?

Here is as good as anywhere, in this lean-to next to the house, with my writing desk and pencils and few sacred objects: a pair of carved immortals, carried here from China, a model Mercer mounted on a black ashtray, missing its driver's seat, the journey over.

An array of photographs: a bearded sailor in tropical whites on the deck of the Comus, somewhere in the Yellow Sea, an old lady with resolute, loving eyes in a familiar chair with her daughters standing behind her. A younger woman by the Town Hall steps, holding up her certificate of naturalisation – a smile charged with southern light. Two brothers in the back yard of a terraced house, giddy with excitement on the older boy's first day at school – the little one in awe of his badge and uniform.

I step outside onto the lawn. High above me, aeroplanes draw intersecting lines against a cloudless sky. A shadow in an upstairs window catches my eye. Yes, I should start here, then work outwards, and backwards.

The Water Tower

In the sky-blue bedroom, a biplane hangs from the ceiling by cotton threads, swaying almost imperceptibly. The golden boy grabs onto the windowsill and lifts himself on tiptoes. His image could be from fifteen years or half a century ago: honey blond hair tapered to a hamster's tail at the nape of his neck, cotton short trousers, ankle socks and buckled shoes. The view from the window unfolds. This is his window and his view, its story told by the old man who once stood here with him.

A lifetime ago, men with spades and pickaxes came to level the land behind the new houses. That's why the gardens stride away down the hillside like the terraces of Machu Picchu. And it's why nothing grows on the high sides where they dug the soil away down to the hard clay. There they built retaining walls with recycled gritstone, filled in behind with broken bricks and concrete rubble – only buddleia davidii's lilac inflorescences bursting through.

In those days the gardens were all alike – a concrete path outside an olive green back door, a wooden bench where a couple could sit in silence with cups of tea, observing a starling with a crooked beak or sparrows flitting in the privet hedge. A rectangle of lawn with a military cut and a standing guard of expertly pruned roses. At the back was a vegetable patch, with bean frames of soldered copper pipe, crops in neat rows and foil strips to scare the birds. A creosoted shed stood there, perhaps containing a lathe and an unfinished model steam train – built by hand, from memory.

When the war came, the old man said, they all built shelters with bags of sand and curved sheets of crinkled steel. That explained the rectangle of refractory bricks, now a dense bed of dandelion, Dragon Heart and Johnson's Blue.

Beyond the terraced gardens a wooded hillside rose in the distance, crowned by a round castle that fascinated the boy and reappeared in his dreams. But it wasn't really a castle, the old man said, it was a water tower (which confused the boy just for a moment, convinced he could see a tower of stone). Standing with him at the window, the old man panned a leathery hand from west to east, writing the landscape's story with his extended finger.

The water was gathered high up on the moors, in the dams at Redmires, he said. From there it flowed down to the city in enormous tubes – he drew their diameters with extended arms – big enough for a boy to crawl through.

The world was like a giant magnet, he said, pulling the water downhill, the same way it pulled the boy's feet to the floor so he didn't float away like a balloon. It pulled the water through pipes all over the city, ready to use when you turned your tap on. But it wouldn't flow up, which was a problem for the people who lived on the hill. So they built a machine to pump it to the top of the stone tower. From there, the magnet pulled it down again, and now they had all the water they could ever want.

And just for fun they built a viewing platform too, so you could climb the tower and see the city stretching out before you – its glinting rivers and high-rises, its valleys and trees and rows of red houses.

The boy imagined the massive pipes coming down from Redmires, big enough for a boy to crawl through. And he imagined he was crawling through them in his shorts, ankle socks and buckled shoes, beneath the feet of other children walking to school. Like his golden hamster, squeezing through plastic tubes in her cylindrical cage, he descended his valley side then ascended the other – without a graze on his knees or a trace of moisture – before reaching the water tower, climbing to the top, and popping out into the sunlight.

As he gazed from his window he waved hesitantly, certain he could see a boy with honey blond hair waving back to him, untroubled by the impossibility of waving to himself across the deep, wooded valley.

Creation Story

It was a quiet Monday evening at the confluence of two rivers – just down the hill from Shoe Zone and the slots and gaming experience. Quiet, that is, until the Sun God, dabbling in his celestial laboratory, sparked a powerful reaction of alchemical elements – primordial earth, water, air and fire.

All at once the city burst into being.

Earth yielded wooded valleys for shelter, fertile fields for sustenance, trees to be coppiced and turned to charcoal – fuel for the city's fires.

Rock formations bore layers of ironstone – loaded with ore to feed the foundries – and fine-grained sandstone – for grinding sharp edges on knife blanks.

Coal measures disgorged the sun's energy, captive for three hundred million years, distilled to near-pure carbon for combustion at two thousand degrees. (Ganister was laid on for furnace linings – to resist the fierce heat.)

Water fell as rain on the hills, rushing in streams down the valley sides, filling fast-flowing rivers to drive hammers and grindstones, granting the city its physical and psychic forms.

Air came as the prevailing wind, scrolling the grey sky relentlessly from west to east, and in the blast, forced through tuyeres to raise the forge's heat.

Fire was everywhere: in the charcoal burners' kilns buried beneath damp clay, in the lead-smelting boles and the blacksmiths' hearths, in the fireboxes, bloomeries and Bessemer converters.

Behdety looked down on his creation and reckoned it was all right. Then, I suppose, he took Anubis for his evening walk – past the park cafe, out along the river, towards the sunset.

A Boy Called Coral

It was something the Matriarch said that set me off – searching for Uncle Coral. We were in the day room of the care home over on Sicey Avenue, huddled around her, talking for her, paying reverence, really. She liked to sit there by the long window, comforted by the familiar view across the estate, clutching the chair's wooden arm with a cannula-bruised hand.

Her condition was confusion, but nothing unusual for ninety-eight. No disease corrupted her character. Her keen eyes still glinted with humour, cutting down condescension with accusatory flashes. The steel core remained intact.

But sleep and therefore dreams dominated her days, dissolving reality, substituting kaleidoscopes of imaginings and memories. Decline, of course, but also something else – a slow return to the infinite, and reunions unbounded by physical bodies. She too had news to relate.

Grandma Clara had been to visit, she said, as though it were unremarkable. Aunt Mabel too – an embassy from a different century, no less. They'd gathered by the fireplace and Grandma had talked about Coral again. He was her favourite, without a doubt.

Gently, with the tip of her left forefinger, she stroked the antique ring on her right middle finger – a serpent coiled around a stone of opaque orange-pink.

∾

A hundred and twenty years before, on her first wedding anniversary, Clara had removed her grandmother's coral ring from its leather box and slipped it onto her own middle finger. Then she touched it and made a wish – that soon she would be in the family way. When her son was born she called him Coral, so he too would be blessed with good fortune.

She was a protective mother with aspirations to respectability, so she was glad when the grown-up lad found work at the new Co-operative store. Far safer than the foundry, she thought, and he looked so smart in his waistcoat and white collar. She believed in social betterment and the movement's stance against 'the tyranny of sweated labour'. They'd treat him well and he was clever – he might even go far.

The scene in my mind is of Coral serving at the counter of a crowded grocery shop. Chipper and charming, sliding and climbing a wooden ladder to grab packets of Silk Cut and SAXA from high shelves, punching the buttons of a baroque National till – its superfluous bronze soon to be melted down for ordnance. Rewarding loyal customers with smiles and chits towards quarterly dividends.

When the war came, and in spite of intense maternal fears, Clara was proud that he was among the first to volunteer. In her mind, belief in King and Empire sat comfortably with a temperate, insular form of socialism. Empire made the city wealthy and could, in turn, fulfil her family's dreams of prosperity.

For Coral, an eighteen-year-old lad fostered with fantasies of dreadnoughts and dragoons, the war promised adventure and glory – a well-timed opportunity to prove his manhood. He enlisted as a private in the local regiment's territorial battalion. After training in Lincolnshire and York they landed at Boulogne in April 1915.

The River - Part One

On Burbage Moor, pure water rises from the earth to gather at the valley head – a land of lonely fieldfare and smiling lama pacos.

A stream forms and finds its flow – tumbling through the wooded clough, cascading over moss-covered gritstone, building velocity – energy for industry in the booming city below.

Before the age of coal, the dams of water mills and grinding hulls multiplied along the river – set in clusters of woods and meadows, a strand of teardrop sapphires and trapezoid emeralds.

The valley's a place for pleasure now – Sunday walks with tea stops at the old forge, revue shows of synchronised dipping mallards, two boys at the big slide seeking speed on polyester coats.

Beyond the bridge a channel steers water away from the brook – through the sluice gate, into the pond, along the rushing goit. An iron wheel still turns there – driving shafts, gears, pulleys and leather belts.

Inside the hull, knife grinders straddled their wooden saddles, hunched over spinning disks of brittle rock. Exposed to exploding wheels and malign silica dust; death riding with them on his pale horse.

Coral's War

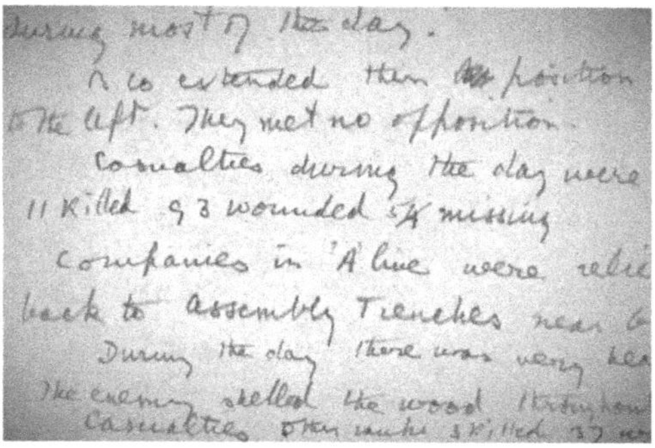
during most of the day.
Co extended their position
to the left. They met no opposition.
Casualties during the day were
11 killed 93 wounded missing
companies in 'A' line were
back to assembly Trenches near
During the day there was very
The enemy shelled the wood
Casualties killed

Familiar images provide that war with definition and perhaps even a macabre sort of meaning: brave, frightened men clambering up ladders, hare-brained attacks across No Man's Land, corpses snagged like rags on barbed wire. But Coral's battalion experienced a different kind of war, at least for the rest of 1915. One history says their role was to 'stand and wait' – a deceptively benign description of daily life in the salient.

Because you could say they experienced the conflict in its essential form – as a grinding, industrial process with a predictable circularity: front line, support line, reserve line, rest in billets behind the lines – cleaning bodies, boots and uniforms. Forward again to the front. Stand to – *the morning hate* – stand down, rations of bacon, tea and rum, kit and rifle maintenance, mud, rats and body lice, stand to, stand down, night work fixing trenches and wire – silhouettes exposed to snipers' bullets.

Seasons turned but without respite: frozen feet and boots in winter, spring bringing forth only toxic mud, hard-baked ground in summer affording no protection – just flies and nauseating putrefaction.

And the final, mandatory stage of death-production: continual decimation by shelling, mechanically cutting away the next slice. A grim output recorded precisely by a bureaucratic mill of equal efficiency, its ontology at the intersection of feudal and machine ages, its tally of waste mingled with cursory meteorological musings:

'Fine day. Lieut. CM D____ killed by a sniper. 3 men killed, 8 wounded.'

'Rained off and on all day.'

'Captain M____ killed when bandaging a wounded man. 13 killed and 35 wounded.'

The men rotated through French villages with Flemish names – Steenvorde, Zutkerque – then into and out of the salient – Elverdinge, Sarragossa Farm.

'Trenches in an awful state,' the battalion diary tells us. 'Heavy bombardment, enemy only shelled us.' Another batch of fresh recruits replaced dead experienced men, this time 'of slightly better physique, but many very young.'

The serpent remained coiled – sleeping.

Purporting to describe how Coral and his comrades felt during those days would be fraudulent, at least for this writer. But we do know that on a single day 'two men accidentally shot themselves' – 'some rain.'

In the spring of 1916 the narrative changes suddenly. Billeted behind the lines in Contay, the men were conditioned to attack – bomb throwing, bayonet fighting, specialist instruction for Lewis gunners. From just six hundred, a few months before, the battalion's strength was back up to a thousand. Fattening the beast.

On 30th June they marched to assembly trenches in Aveluy Wood, burdened with the paraphernalia of offensive warfare: bombs, sandbags, extra rounds of ammunition, rations for two days in hostile territory.

Then, on 1st July, the 'Big Push' began. As to progress: 'contrary reports were received.'

On 2nd July, orders came to hold the old front line around Thiepval Wood. Shelling. 15 other ranks killed, 88 wounded.

The entry for Monday 3rd July alludes to chaos in a storm of steel. Forward troops isolated, communications disrupted – 'casualties to runners' – ration-carrying parties scattered by shrapnel.

'The company holding the old front line was heavily shelled most of the day.'

It was there that the bastard snake roused and uncoiled itself, raising its head from the dirt of Thiepval Wood, guiding the devil's artillery down onto Coral's position. By the day's end, one officer and eleven men had been killed, ninety-three wounded. Five men were missing – a four is crossed out with a neat diagonal line.

I speculate, grasping at straws. Could Coral have been the fifth missing man? And could that officer's pen stroke embody specific knowledge, and therefore a kind of memory, of his fate? A forgotten man's death infused with gravity by a deliberate, dedicated act, however minuscule?

Coral's name is memorialised, of course – on a Celtic cross by the road at Wadsley Bridge, at Skew Hill cemetery on the Co-operative Society obelisk, on the vast Thiepval Memorial in Picardy, in the regimental book in the cathedral chapel, locked inside a glass case.

None of which has much to do with remembering – only with the fact that cold, silent stone is easier to honour than living, breathing men. We're only touched by Coral's humanity when we read the proforma letter from the War Office: personal articles belonging to the deceased, it decrees, should be sent to Clara. It's for us to imagine his grieving mother at the moment of unwrapping them.

The City Battalion

The Duke's interest in the city ran deep. (He owned half its land and the mineral wealth beneath). So when war was declared and the call came to serve, it was he, naturally, who took the lead.

With vicarious valour he pledged a unit of superior men – bankers, students, teachers and lawyers – in defence of his realm. Crackling with excitement or just carried along, a thousand of them volunteered.

They enrolled in a Town Hall reception room – a line of recruits advancing up the grand marble staircase. The Duke received them himself, praising their spirit in equally splendid verbiage.

Later they were summoned to the Corn Exchange – the registry of births and deaths – to swear allegiance to the King.

Training commenced at Edmund Road barracks and in the old deer park (both, incidentally, bearing the Duke's name). Just a game of soldiers at first, in civvies with puttees and outmoded rifles.

Billets were at Redmires Camp, high above the city. They're still there in sepia photographs: company set-pieces with solemn faces or joshing after days of labour – shirtless, smiling, shovel-wielding ghosts.

On Quarry Hill, in sleet and hail, they cut trenches with fire steps and parapets. Even today they scar the ground like Nazca geoglyphs

– twisted, tormented beings, overtures to alien, less warlike civilisations.

In spring, the battalion marched down to Midland Station, cheered on by citizens with paper flags. After Cannock and Salisbury Plain they sailed for Alexandria, and a fight with the Turk that never took place.

The voyage might have been traced on a boy's map of Empire – a red line and a ship of the line passing legendary locations – Barrosa, Trafalgar and Valetta's Grand Harbour, criss-crossed by gondolas in the sunshine.

Egypt ran its film reel of oriental fantasy: fellahin in turbans and dazzling jalabiya, camel train silhouettes against desert skies. Then the finery of Port Said, where English ladies welcomed them with cups of tea.

A change of plan moved the grand tour to France – landing at Marseille, a train ride through the Rhône from Arles to Mâcon. But Dijon station was a brutal awakening – platforms strewn with men disfigured at Verdun.

Moving to the front the soldiers crossed familiar thresholds – from innocence to experience, youth to manhood, pastoral perfection to a barren zone of transition, then onward to a realm of danger and chaos.

But this would be no mythical heroes' tale, the story's arc would be violently cut short. In France there would be no great trial and overcoming, only weeks of attrition and a sudden mass-death event.

And afterwards there would be no triumphant return to the city – just cynicism and a century of clichés: the faulty barrage, the uncut wire, the sad, slow walk up the hill.

By 3rd July, when the battalion left the line – the day Coral met his maker on the other side of the Ancre – most of the men were dead or wounded.

'Two years in the making,' somebody wrote afterwards, 'ten minutes in the destroying.'

Roman Ridge Trilogy

Brigantia

Family oral history tells us we're the progeny of shopkeepers, bricklayers, musicians and yo-yo demonstrators, but how far can we imagine our roots descending into the city's earth?

I walk with the boy – a man now – up a gradual incline and along an ancient track, following a ridgeline honed by embankments built in the time of Claudius. One story says this was a defensive line connecting Iron Age hill forts to the north and south-west of the city. Our objective is a third, mid-way between the others, holding out among the housing and industry.

Centuries of exploitation have eroded and exhausted this landscape. Thickets of gorse, tipped with yellow flowers, hide quarry workings and spoil heaps. Stunted birch trees struggle in the stony ground. At the brow of the hill a gap in the trees reveals a vista of the East End: the foundries, forges and machine shops of the River Don Works, lined up like formations of basalt, the sprawling shopping vortex where East Hecla used to stand, the dismal complex of multi-screen cinema, fast food franchises and development corporation conflicts of interest, countless metal boxes containing car showrooms, gearbox gurus, plate rollers and precision grinders.

To the north and west the city's suburbs extend into the distance: the Flower Estate and the General Hospital, Corporation street patterns flowing like biological organisms, the school that bore a duke's title until it was named and shamed for poor performance (I imagine a polite but potent word in the relevant ear – the withdrawal of naming rights).

The hill fort itself isn't much to see – a shallow, elliptical ditch with the excavated earth piled up on the outer side. This defensive counterscarp was found to be faced with vitrified stone, melted and fused at more than a thousand degrees – either inspired, early military tech or evidence that our antecedents, too, took heat from belligerent southerners. From more recent history we find patches of burnt gorse trimmed with crushed lager cans. The impulse to burn stuff runs deep here.

The *fort* denomination is, it seems, presumptive – no one really knows what function this place served – military, mercantile or spiritual? But for a certain kind of provincial romantic it's a portal to another world – of animistic magic with white robes, golden sickles and mistletoe, and plucky resistance against powerful enemies.

I want to believe this was part of a mighty bulwark built by a tribe of northern Britons against invaders from the south – Roman legions in this case. It fits a certain narrative, and besides, the historical details are irresistible.

In the years of the Roman conquest, Queen Cartimandua of the Brigantes sided, unforgivably, with the empire. But her ex, Venutius, wasn't with the programme, so he took up arms against her and her imperial overlords. (Cartimandua had dumped him for his younger armour-bearer, Vellocatus, whose name meant *better in battle*. We can assume it was a messy divorce). Vanutius's initially domestic quest for revenge led to him becoming king and a continual irritant to the Romans, until the point at which he disappears from the records – possibly consigned to a subterranean hole wearing the first-century equivalent of a bright orange suit.

We rely on our creative imaginations to picture characters from the lines of Tacitus (not to mention this libidinous mess of power, war and sex). In mine, Cartimandua is alluring, Venutius somewhat ridiculous, with a jealous sneer and cuckold's horns. And yet, as a rebel instigator of guerilla war against an almighty hegemon, I feel compelled to take his side.

Standing on this hill, mobilising meticulously cultivated identity and prejudice, it's a joy to indulge fantasies of fearless continuity from these ancient antecedents, manning the fused-stone ramparts against onslaughts out of the sun: Romans, Angles, harrying Normans, a distant government's brutal militia, the Imperial Treasury's punitive austerity. The sense of siege is intensified by traces of anti-aircraft batteries and barrage balloon anchors – built for defence against Zeppelins then, later, Messerschmitts and Heinkels. You can add the Germans to that list, too.

But the truth of this place is less binary, and, for some, no doubt, more unsettling. For this has always been border territory – a place where battles were fought with external foes but also where identities melded.

People here will bristle at the question even being asked, then place themselves firmly on one side of a clear dividing line: North versus South, North versus Midlands, Tyke versus Ram, Tyke versus everyone, Elmet then Northumbria against Mercia, Maxima against Flavia Caesariensis, Brigantia against Rome and its Corieltauvian minions.

But, in fact, the historical border ran through the modern city, not around it, and this assertively northern metropolis incorporates vast areas which, until recently, were possessions of the Midlands – that semi-southern realm of the Car Park King where, we like to think, hands and vowels are lower down the Rockwell scale than our own.

Even as I write this, the local newspaper is reporting (or manufacturing?) public outrage at a suggestion that this might be a Mercian city – too painful, too close to the bone. Yet for some this frontier location is key to understanding the city's distinctive identity

– peripherality, an outsider quality, recalcitrance towards remote centres of power and authority. That works for me, but, then, I'm compromised, having spent a lifetime running the border – a potential fifth columnist to be treated with suspicion, not completely 'one of us.'

Intersection

Beyond the fort, on the south side of the hill, the path descends through the woods and terminates at a gap in the ridge. Terraced houses and a Jamaican restaurant line a three-way intersection – once a bustling bottleneck where manpower funnelled from the northern estates to the factories of the East End.

The road rises and turns to the west, following the route of the ancient track. We pass the Wesleyan Reform Chapel, its sandstone blackened by a century of pollution, then a diminutive Kingdom Hall, then the mass of the new Grand Mosque. Purveyors of paradise clustered like car dealerships, divine redemption to your own custom specification.

The road along the ridge leads us through a dilapidated, liminal landscape: collapsing walls of stone and brick fragments thrown together in distant centuries, timeworn Victorian villas with litter-strewn gardens, decades old temporary security fencing, splayed limbs of buddleia davidii taunting us from waste ground.

Three massive care home blocks loom into view, six storeys high by fifty windows wide, like a mega cruise ship washed up on the escarpment's rocks at the end of the final show. The style: Insane Asylum Revival – red brick, inevitably, attic rooms with undersized fenestration for the most troublesome (or least lucrative) inmates. At the back the terrain falls away – a reminder of the ridge's artificiality – leading down to forgotten plots of fly-tipped scrubland.

In the valley below we see remnants of the city's steel-making canyons. Beyond are the scrap metal yards, warrens of fabrication shops and recycling plants of Salmon Pastures – once a salubrious bend in the river.

It was somewhere around here, on a gloomy night more than a hundred years ago, that a Zeppelin's flight path penetrated the defensive line of the Brigantes.

The Blue Light

The Imperial Navy airship – tactical number L-22 – set out from Germany on the afternoon of 25th September 1916. It was a craft of immense proportions – sixty feet in diameter by almost six hundred in length – held aloft by hydrogen and propelled by a quartet of six-cylinder Maybach engines. The suspended gondolas housing its crew were paradigms of Machine Age futurism: melees of gauges, pipes and esoteric mechanisms, aluminium panels and struts with rows of raised rivets, an incongruous ship's wheel with turned wooden handles. Vertiginous complexity.

The pilot crossed the coast near Mablethorpe, setting his course by the resort town. About an hour later he approached the city from the south-east, following a circular flightpath – north over Redmires then to starboard, cruising above the western suburbs.

"Suddenly we heard a droning, terrifying sound overhead, which came stronger every minute." – Eyewitness account, 25th September 1916.

In the city below electric air raid buzzers sounded their warnings. Terrified citizens fled to the illusory safety of woods and parks. The airship zig-zagged to evade the expected onslaught of shells and bullets. But not a shot was fired from Wincobank fort, nor from any of the city's other hilltop air defence positions. According to unofficial accounts – made piquant, no doubt, by popular prejudice – the officers in charge were otherwise engaged, attending a ball at the Grand Hotel in town.

Shortly after midnight the Zeppelin dropped its first bombs near the entrance to Burngreave Cemetery. Then more were disgorged onto a concentration of slums to the east of the ridge – home to some of the city's poorest inhabitants.

Out of an opaque night sky, war visited sudden death upon the city. A man was killed in his bed by shrapnel, another almost decapitated. A grandmother's back was torn open by a bomb fragment, nearly slicing her in two. She died later in hospital but her grandchild was unharmed. In one street alone four homes were destroyed with families inside them – grandparents, parents and their children.

In a row of tidy terraced houses to the east of the cemetery, overlooking the locus of destruction, I see a young woman staring from a bay window – a silhouette of bishop sleeves and pompadour hair. Motionless, as though turned to stone, she might be experiencing *'the strangest sense of detachment'* from the world about her, seeming to *'watch it all from the outside, from somewhere inconceivably remote.'* [1]

She's alone in the house, just her and the children. Her husband, a teacher by profession, is away at the war. He was still alive on the 17th, the date of his last letter. But now, once again, his existence is suspended. Below her the infernos and smokestacks of a mechanised Hades stretch away across the valley. The groans and screams of corrupted machines lacerate the night.

The years of her youth saw the old world obliterated by scientific and technological revolution: the disorienting magic of electricity and electromagnetic waves, the appearance, against nature, of

---

1 HG Wells, *The War of the Worlds*, 1898

automobiles and flying machines, the rock of her Methodist communion with God fractured by rumours of His death.

And now the world's capacity for ingenious invention, production and progress has been honed and harnessed only to the destruction of human life. Like everyone in this grief-wracked city her nerves are torn to pieces – traumatised by total war, tales of bestial enemies and imminent invasion, the absence of all the men, the daily, cursory letters telling of their wastage on the Somme, the muffled screams of wives and mothers behind closed doors.

"I saw it. A reddish flash at the edge, the slightest projection of the outline just as the chronometer struck midnight…" HG Wells, The War of the Worlds, 1898.

The popular literature of the era, well-thumbed on their own bookshelves, portended this night, warning of a world-beating Empire's ultimate vulnerability, war in the air, an alien race with overwhelming innovations attacking from the sky. Outside her window the leviathan looms over a city on the brink of psychological collapse – vast, other-worldly, menacing and nauseous in the soft glow of its blue light – a final, dystopian signal.

"He had a blue light on the front of his machine, glaring enough to blind you, and as the machine moved away, and the glare passed, the outlines of the airship could be seen!" – Eyewitness account, 25th September 1916.

And we should remember: it was only known later that the airship had come alone. For the people who saw it there might have been a vast flotilla, ready to disgorge cylinders loaded with mythical, murderous men and invincible weapons.

From the things she saw that night, a different woman – her identity unknown – was reported to have 'lost it,' running along a devastated street, screaming, before being dragged into the relative safety of a building. These were human minds at their limits, stretched to their yield points – the point beyond which permanent deformation occurs.

The Zeppelin raid – now largely forgotten in the city – destroyed eighty-nine houses and killed twenty-nine people. Today it requires unusual curiosity to hunt down their graves at Burngreave, or, further along the path of destruction, the memorial stone on the Baltic Works' perimeter wall.

On Princess Street the Primitive Methodist Chapel was destroyed in the raid. Afterwards, the building's only surviving wall continued to bear these words:

A new commandment I give unto you, that ye love one another.

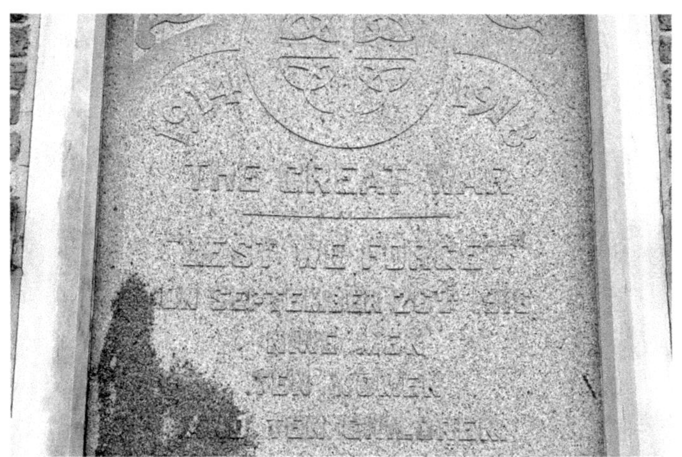

View from the Cliffe

The woman I now think of as the Matriarch was born in the spring of the war's final year. The old world was nearing its expiry date, the Romanovs and the Austro-Hungarian empire still existed – just. Zeppelins had ceased to stalk the city's skies, but a more deadly threat hung in the air.

She was, in her own words, 'born on the wrong side of the sheets.' So I suspect the christening in the diminutive chapel was only lightly attended by a smattering of embarrassed shopkeepers, traders and metalworkers of the more respectable sort. The house of God I'm conjuring echoes with splutters and sneezes, the dearly beloved sharing the novel microbe munificently – the allegedly Spanish flu.

The infant girl is at the front by the baptismal font – cradled in a minister's pasty arms, immobilised in an abundant white gown, biting chunks out of putrid air. Trialling an early prototype of *that look* – a fusion of wide-eyed goodness and the impact resistance of tool steel.

Because of the unplanned nature of the conception and, I suspect, the cluelessness of the kids involved, she was raised by her maternal grandparents – musicians who together owned and ran a shop on the Common. While Grandad taught violin in the back room, Grandma Kitty ran the commercial operation – selling instruments and sheet music, later complemented by gramophones and records.

The Matriarch claimed to have been the city's first disc jockey – plugging the latest hit songs under Grandma's expert tutelage, cranking up the machine and directing its fluted horn towards the wedged-open shop door.

Beneath skies burdened with the darkest clouds of depression, in a drop-waist dress and a bob cropped to the earlobes, she'd tout for custom from the Common's passing footfall: sweaty steelmen and jobless stragglers, office clerks from accounts or exports, typing pool girls with spare money – still living at home, a war veteran on crutches in a suit with a singular trouser. Her sparkling eyes and broad grin no doubt proved irresistible to those with the means and a fair few without, spreading a little happiness with Binnie Hale over the racket of foundry trucks, drop hammers and squealing tramcars.

Her world was a labyrinth of blackened terraced houses and cobbled back roads – Clarefield, Melville, Ravensworth, Campbell – set between mile-long mills that roared and exhaled steam and smoke. She felt safe in these tight-knit streets, with a woman in every home and domestic life spilling out onto stone pavements. There were unsavoury sorts, of course – the sordid old men who loitered by the urinal on the corner of Terry Street. But they kept their hands to themselves, knowing they were in the crosshairs of a thousand pairs of watchful eyes. Still, it was a hard and sometimes brutal place – just living here sharpened your wits and toughened your hide.

The shop was barely a minute's walk from school – just the other side of Carltonville Road from the gate pier carved with the word *Girls*. After tidying the breakfast table and washing the pots she'd wait in her attic window, captivated by the costumes of passers-by in the street below. When the bell sounded in its high gable she'd be off, dashing down the stairs and out of the shop door, Grandma shouting warnings after her. The challenge, the imperative – to arrive just before the ringing stopped.

The gennels between the rows of houses were her playground – for kicking balls against looming walls or bowling at stumps painted on the backs of outhouses. The only girl in a gang of good lads, immersed in their rugged street life and vernacular. At tea time she'd head back to the warmth and serenity of the closed shop, with Grandad in his corner chair, playing Purcell.

She was drawn to the boys' games, recognising no limits. But she was only three when the men of the Association stole football from the women. In a world of more confident males she might have been a solid centre back for the midweek team, her skills honed by 'football amazon' alumni from the projectile factories, instilling fear into the mighty Preston Ladies.

The slice of territory Grandad allowed her to roam was bounded by Abyssinia Bridge, the river and the railway line, beyond which lay a perilous man's world of steelworks, hard-drinking pubs, waste ground and the deadly, black soup of the canal. To the south-west she could venture further, along the main road as far as Christ Church and the cemetery – a verdant island in a landscape the colour of lignite.

There they'd play hide and seek behind elaborate tombs and headstones, beneath yew trees and menacing lancet windows, observing in fascination the residents of this avian haven: gaggles of excitable sparrows, magpies in numbers that told fortunes, blackbirds exposed by yellow beaks among the mouse ear and flatweed – vegetation as indestructible as everything else here.

From the church yard they'd skip along the cemetery path, down the slope to the bend in the river that flowed gently but irrepressibly, speaking its stories in hushed tones. There, in the shadow of Hecla, they'd throw stones from the cliff that seemed so high, aiming at the arches of tail goits on the other side. Then they'd sprint off towards the lattice bridge and Liverpool Street, heading for home.

The men, it seemed, had forgotten to stop her swimming, so she decided to excel at it. At least twice a week she'd visit the public baths across the road from Christ Church, ploughing lines of front crawl, then backstroke, then breaststroke, her technique admired by watchers on the balcony or exiting their cubicles, the pool a Roman spa lined with Corinthian columns.

When she started work and had money to spend, the baths yielded another joy: washing in comfort and privacy – impossible in the tin bath at home. The ritual itself evoked a frisson of adult pleasure: paying at the kiosk for a numbered ticket, a fresh, folded towel and a fragment of soap, waiting on the bench in anticipation of the indulgence to come, luxuriating in piping-hot water in a vast slipper bath and a steam-soaked cubicle. There she'd stretch out her arms and legs in a flamboyant, womanly manner, cleansing herself with the best lather a feeble soap bar could muster, repressing giggles as the leading lady bathing beyond the wall belted out show songs with steamy theatricality:

'Can't help lovin' dat man of mine

When he goes away-ee, that's a rainy day-ee …'

Leaving school at the age of fourteen, in the depths of the depression, she was the only girl in her class to find a job. Grandma's instruction in the art of enticing customers had served her well. Now she could hone her talents in a magical world of dolls houses and Dinkys, Meccano sets and circulating model trains, swinging and spinning yo-yos at the entrance to Wilson Gumpert's toy shop.

(One thing leads to another – from there it was just a short walk across Fitzalan Square to her next place of employment – the telephone exchange at the General Post Office, where she would work during the war).

At fifteen, her world changed abruptly. Grandma was the last of the couple to die. The music shop closed then ceased to exist, with little to show for their years in commerce. Violins were hard to shift in the early thirties.

For a young woman whose life would come to resemble a series of discrete acts in an absorbing play, the scenery turned and a different set appeared: the new Corporation estate at Shiregreen and her parents' house on Sicey Avenue. She adapted with barely a comment. It was called 'getting on with it,' she said, back in the day.

Thursday 12th

It starts with a clear, motionless image – a composite assembled from imaginings and old photos in the family horror box. A young woman in the kitchen at Mason Lathe Road, seen in profile against the ceiling lamp's glow. Tumbling, shoulder-length auburn curls, piled up on top with bobby pins and side combs. A rejuvenated fantasy of the older face I knew – Bergman-inspired but earthier, radiating love and mischief.

A slender version of her hand takes a glass from the draining board, dries it with a tea towel, then places it in the pale-yellow cabinet. Then a second glass and a pair of dinner plates painted with calendula flowers. They've eaten tea together, unusually in silence. Afterwards her husband of just a year hurried out into a cold night glistening with frost, illuminated by a near-full moon.

From the front room the wireless carried uplifting announcements in clipped, officer-class diction, typically unacquainted with doubt. Victory in Sidi Barrani – a significant Egyptian town. Combined arms operating in flawless unison – another nail in the Axis coffin. Chaos drawn with a coherent, bold outline – a single panel ready, one day, to take its place in the war's epic comic strip. A version of the news followed in another alien tongue, sounding, she thought, like a Geordie after one too many.

The seven o'clock slot brought *Howdy Folks!* – comedy with Kenway and Young. But this evening's performance would begin with an unscheduled duet. Just as the show started, the city received a red warning to take cover. A vast formation of bombers was approaching from the south-east.

Siren moans melded with the nasal whine of Mrs Yatton – landlady at the Startled Hare – to produce a heinous polyphony. Dissonant noises laminated: the bass drum of anti-aircraft guns, rising in volume as batteries joined in – Norton Lees, Manor Lane, Parkwood

Springs – tracking the attack towards the north-west. The snare rattle of autocannons repeating.

Mr Grice smacked his lips. 'Very tasty, very sweet'.

In the gardens outside, commotion reigned as parents herded kids between privet hedges towards untested Andersons.

'Keith, you little bugger, get in that shelter…'

Then the guns on Wincobank Hill opened up. The maddening, mechanical drone of massed aero engines crescendoed overhead, assaulting the brain, overwhelming neural switchboards.

Kate grasped the kitchen table top and closed her eyes – sucking in courage, expelling fear through pursed lips, feeling her heart racing, thoughts flickering chaotically.

Shit, he's out in it!

Did Mum and Dad get to the shelter?

Have I got time to change these knickers? (The pair she was wearing had a split seam – a disgrace in the likely event of her night ending at the infirmary).

Stay calm. Think. Remember the plan they'd worked out together.

Based on a shared, supernatural insight that their love nest was invulnerable, they'd decided to build their refuge in the house, not in the garden. Then they'd considered and rejected the Morrison – a reinforced table with caged sides and a double bed underneath. Not a chance – too much like a rabbit hutch, none of the potential for physical passion. Finally, they'd settled on the alcove under the stairs where a frayed armchair cushion now awaited her. In a model of time and motion she assembled the survival kit, her own innovation: a bottle of Guinness grabbed from the pantry, two Player's cigarettes from the kitchen cabinet, a copy of *Woman* from the drop-leaf table, the cardboard box containing her gas mask – for use only in desperation. Then an unplanned interlude – the fast, artful application of red lipstick in front of the fantail mirror.

As prepared as possible she squeezed herself into a den already provisioned with matches, candles, a Bakelite ashtray and a Tennant Brothers bottle opener.

Perfect timing. At the moment her backside hit the cushion a landmine detonated somewhere near the main road. Cardboard-covered glass clattered in the windows but refused to shatter. She lit and drew deeply on a cigarette, then exhaled, pumping her curled tongue against her top lip, focusing on the smoke rings that expanded then diffused. The night outside was a bedlam of bomb blasts and defensive fire. Explosions were sharp and expansive or terse and muffled, as though constrained inside sealed containers. Thuds, rattles and machine gun trills emanated from the hill. Overhead the enemy persisted. Death was close by and in the distance, and always, potentially, coming for her next.

Screaming and losing it, taking refuge in temporary dissolution, was an option she considered consciously. But instead, with eyes closed, she maintained focus on a point in front of her, implementing a kind of internal escape.

It was their wedding day. Her little sister, the bridesmaid, sulking in a crown of flowers and a layered dress; paper confetti floating to the ground, watched through a white veil. A sunlit morning in May on Filey Beach, touched by a cool breeze, their bare feet sinking into warm sand. The day they met outside the shops at the Circle – groceries for Mum in a string bag, his gentle humour and kind eyes.

Hours passed and the sounds of the raid receded. By nine o'clock there were only rumbles in the distance off to the south, barely audible over the chimes of Big Ben. Kate remained in the refuge, waiting for the all-clear, but the moments of greatest risk had passed – others were in danger now.

Soothing music filtered through – a film score cue for the calm that inevitably follows action. Her face relaxed into a slight smile. Her head swayed, humming, lightly intoxicated. The String Quintet in C major – familiar, if not by name. One of Grandma's favourites.

Her eyes shot open.

'Well I never!' she said, out loud.

'Beethoven. They're playing bloody Beethoven!'

It was late – the early hours of Friday 13th. The fight was over but still the city awaited the siren's continuous note. Kate was shattered, the adrenaline syringed out of her. She wanted to wait up for him but knew she wouldn't stay awake – he'd be out all night. And she sensed that he was safe, as though her thoughts had sustained him, wrapping a protective blanket around him. She took a second bottle of stout from the pantry and carried it upstairs – to knock out the night.

The River – Part Two

The river runs on through the valley parks, past a Spion Kop of daffodils in spring and stubs of rhododendron in winter, bloodied by transfusions from iron-laden tributaries.

It flows between the stepping stones where we fished for trout with home-made rods, by the rockabilly roundabout where the boys rode fibreglass cars, past the playground where rats snack on sandwich crusts.

In summer, the park field releases its unique pheromone – a blend of dog shit, dope and instant barbecues. Kids sit in circles sharing music, chat and own-label lager. A burning yellow bin drips plastic lava.

The old queen surveys the scene with stony disapproval – not amused by this unbroken city of layabouts and rebels.

Friday 13th

At seven, the alarm clock's trill only partially broke through. Still half asleep, Kate reached out to where he should have been but felt only a cold bedsheet. He hadn't come home. The realisation jolted her like an electric shock. She leapt from the bed and bounded down the stairs, almost falling, colliding with the banister. He was there in the front room, slumped in the armchair, still wearing blue overalls smeared with dirt and masonry dust, the cuts on his hands sealed with dried blood. She pressed two fingers against his wrist to find his pulse. Just to be sure. Then she kissed him gently on the cheek and placed a cushion beside his head. Now she could leave him be.

She got ready for work in a hurry – a wash with a flannel in front of the sink, hastily applied hair clips and lipstick, two snatched slices of bread with marmalade for breakfast. She couldn't be late, not today. And who knew how long it would take to reach the telephone exchange?

Outside, the morning was cold and bright, the sun a perfect white disk behind a muslin shroud. Already the streets were humming with voices and activity – excitement still eclipsing the war's burgeoning tragedy. On Bellhouse Road soldiers guarded a gap in the houses where a landmine had detonated – the rubble remains of a family home. Crowds of commercial workers strode southwards towards the city centre, some with their heads down, denying the chaos all around them, others sharing urgent information – casualties, the locations of incidents, the news that none of the buses or tramcars were running.

At Shiregreen Lane a gang of factory lads, running late, peeled off towards the East End. A family of somnambulists, bombed-out from the Flower Estate, propelled their remaining belongings in the wreckage of a pram. At the junction with Primrose Avenue, Kate crouched down to adjust the heel of a new Oxford shoe, its stiff leather chafing and obsessing her – ridiculous, she tutted, with a war on. Then she carried on down the hill, scrutinised by women in housecoats from bay windows.

At Firth Park shops a disconcerting normality prevailed – the orderly grocer with the precision side parting, polishing and stacking apples under his awning, the pork butcher's wife stretching to hang sausages and black pudding in her window. While the world ended, traders fussed over displays of comic books and bike parts, jars of pickle and bottles of local spicy sauce. Only the downcast walkers and trams accumulating at the terminus were reminders of a ruptured reality.

Without conscious intent, Kate turned left at the intersection, onto the park road, between steep-gabled villas and the bowling green where future battles would unfold. Perhaps she hoped to find peace there, detached from time on an avenue of leafless sycamores and horse chestnuts, sheltered between the woods and the rising park field, running gloved fingers over cast iron railings, distracted by the satisfying vibration. At the foot of the hill the pavilion clock tower reassured with its rock-solid presence. Up ahead Trinity's slender spire marked the next way point, guiding her onwards.

Outside St Cuthbert's the road was strewn with black shards of shrapnel – the devil's confetti. A skinny lad darted between kerbstones, collecting choice pieces in his duffle coat pockets – newly wealthy in this child's hard currency. Cuddy looked on from his high, square tower – more trouble at the kingdom's southern periphery. Was there nowhere he could find peace?

The bombs had spared the main road but still the scene described a state of emergency: abandoned trams and buses, ARP ambulances screeching and rattling towards the City General. By the time she reached Abbeyfield Park, Kate was wincing with a ripped blister. That bloody stone wall seemed to stretch on forever.

Near the Toll Bar there were signs of bomb damage – houses with broken windows and displaced roof tiles. But it was only a foretaste of what lay ahead. Burngreave had suffered again – villas demolished by high explosives, collapsed walls exposing sagging floors, disarranged beds and dressing tables – spilling the secrets of private worlds. Firemen in glinting Carthaginian helmets grappled with leaking hoses, jetting water onto charred wooden beams and superheated bricks. St Catherine watched it all through her white rose window – a Byzantine beauty weeping in pity.

Below Spital Hill, Wicker was a chaos of destruction and debris: dissected tram bodies, tangles of contact and catenary wires, scattered incendiary sticks, some made safe beneath sandbags. Outside Osborn's, an abyss had opened in the road. The picture house was disfigured, the front of the motor garage blown out. Without detonating a bomb had penetrated the bridge's main arch, opening a portal onto the smoke-stained sky. Underneath, only the chassis remained of another luckless tramcar.

Kate pressed on, single-minded in her mission, crossing Lady's Bridge and ascending Waingate, hopscotch hopping between fire hoses drawing water from the river, her sinuses inflamed by air sullied with explosives. At the top of Exchange Street a policeman snarled and jabbed his finger, ordering pedestrians to turn back. Behind him the optician's was still burning, the Co-operative building reduced to ruins.

She stopped suddenly, breathing heavily, staring straight ahead, viewing the scene as though from a point somewhere behind and above her, unable to process the precipitous transformation of a familiar environment. She was fixated on the view through to Angel Street – it shouldn't be possible. A cratered island of desolation lay in between – fragments of chimney breasts and distorted joists, water gushing from shattered mains.

The jewellery store with its shimmering curved windows, crowned by the Duke's coat of arms, was no longer there. She would never stand there again, captivated by rows of chiming clocks and unreachable diamond and pearls. The travel tours shop was gone, its sun-saturated posters for exotic steam cruises torn to pieces. Crossley's drapery had disappeared, so too the fine frontage of Cockayne's department store.

On High Street, crippled tramcars lined up with their windows smashed. Soldiers and workmen were clearing the road, hauling detritus onto the back of a Bedford truck. Further up, Walsh's store was a blackened shell, its Parisian lights and glass facade in pieces on the pavement.

Workers from offices and shops huddled together, shaken, mumbling, speculating, the leaning wall of C&A Modes looming over them. At the corner of Fitzalan Square a solitary arch protruded from a pile of rubble. A disparate group of men – bus driver, bank manager, soldier, coal haulier – struggled to extract a long, unwieldy object from a destroyed cellar.

Kate rushed across the road from Haymarket, still in time for the start of her shift. All around her the city was a montage of moving, misplaced fragments, as though seen through a shattering mirror: pieces of Deco pilasters and oak display cabinets, twisted cables and deformed steel structures. A headless torso and a severed leg, still wearing a burgundy slingback. She shuddered to a halt, dysphagic, nearly retching, before recognising the fractured plaster of dismembered shop mannequins.

For a moment there was relief – everything here was unreal, some kind of exercise or dress rehearsal. But then she saw the sight she would relate sixty years later, its sordid details scarring her memory: rows of lifeless bodies, some on stretchers, half-covered with woollen blankets, others just laid there in bloodied suits, skirts or nightdresses. On the pavement, outside the Marples Hotel.

Ring Road Cycle

St Vincent's

The city changes, endlessly. On Tenter Street only one ragged plot remains – a fenced off plantation of lanky, lilac buddleia davidii. A fractured factory floor, sandstone blocks and half bricks, terracotta rubble in a clay matrix, Co-op bottles and chip trays. Alpro. Strongbow. Monster. Triple Mango Vape. Soon a tower will rise here too, its record-breaking height set to obscure St Vincent's prosthetic belfry ('of great townscape value', according to Pevsner).

Ascending Garden Street – I pass the Chinese Kitchen and the Balti House, the works that makes scissors as desirable as Swiss watches, the Settlement with its grimy rose window, where wiry lads battered suede punchbags and do-gooders rescued poor (and therefore wayward) girls through hygiene and bible classes. The National School clock looms in its grand pediment – 'turn up on time, or else'. A greasy spoon smeared with knifed plaster hangs red lanterns with golden logograms. A block of student cells chases the same demographic, softening hard surfaces with stuffed giant pandas.

Fragments of the old city survive here: three-storey tenements with six-over-six windows, their symmetry unsettled by wonky lintels; stone gateways leading to interior yards that once thrummed with industry. It was to a house somewhere here – near the research institute with growling fans and council-flat decks – that a mission of three Irish priests came a hundred and seventy years ago. Ministering to distressed compatriots, delivering them from evil in a country lost to the true church, received by a grovelling indigent with a leg of mutton and a looking glass. The inscription on the presbytery tells their story: *Evangelizare pauperibus misit me.*

At the brow of Garden Street I look left towards the bulwark of Edward Street flats. Bomb-resistant, defending the summit with barred, turreted stairwells and towering chimney stacks. Luxury replacement accommodation for an immigrant slum population. The wheel turns. Today's comers arrive from further afield – the children of high-rolling patsies in a grand, global education swindle. Provisioned from dayglow corner shops with Sun Moon Lake black tea and signature brown sugar bubble milk – products endorsed by a sinister lucky cat with green laser beam eyes.

Their meeting place is the old St Vincent's church, repurposed now as a 'social hub' with pastel sofas and ping-pong, the mosaic creations of Italian artisans enduring on the walls. A stripped stone altar still stands in the chancel, overseen by a pair of carved angels who might have witnessed a moving, emigre wedding back in the fifties.

It's almost impossible to believe – the term-time population notwithstanding – that the streets around here once bustled with families, traders and industrial workers. That in a previous turn of the wheel the outlines of mediaeval crofts lent their form to a labyrinth of courtyards, smithies and ale shops. Hardly a trace of that world remains. Cheap, mid-century factories, topped out with asbestos, rose up on the same irregular plots. Now they stand vacant and disintegrating, their windows smashed like cartoons, sealed with wire mesh and emblazoned with warning signs:

UNSAFE BUILDING. RISK OF DEATH. KEEP OUT!

The sites in between, cleared for new construction, overwhelm with health and safety advice: wear boots, hard hats and high-vis vests, watch out for trucks and overhead loads, report accidents, report to the site office, reverse with supervision. Children – Don't Play Here! (Appended on the optimistic assumption that the district's juvenile delinquents will read that far).

At the perimeters of derelict plots, where litter-picking liabilities are subject to contractual disputes, there's detritus in fantastical forms and megacity volumes: discarded traffic cones, gas cylinders and pop cans, the fly-tipped contents of an entire suburban garage: lawnmower, strimmer, child's car seat, self-disassembled furniture. At the junction of Snow Lane I'm greeted with a dystopian Christmas card scene: a solitary robin moaning in a barren tree trimmed with wind-blown strands of white foam packaging.

Pockets of the old industries persist like a desert biome: indestructible non-destructive testers, mislaid metallurgy labs, mild steel flange and bracket distributors, powered by a groaning substation marked with the silhouette of a dead man. Struck down by a bolt of lightning. Now they're caught up in their own maelstrom of demolition and replacement, with a new kind of Brass Foundry – fitted out with cinema, gym and air hockey tables. The industry: scrutinising textbooks and tapping keyboards. Manufacturing a new kind of Master.

At the top of Furnace Hill I pause to absorb the view over the Island: rows of eco-homes with grey plastic cladding, the museum with the engine that nimbly changes direction, the mattress showroom and the megachurch – secure behind God's battlements. The tavern where old lads debate the merits of New World IPAs and old-world porters.

I wind my way down to Upper Allen Street where, the records suggest, my ancestors lived a century and a half ago: a cutler and his family in a meagre court dwelling, perhaps with a forge in a lean-to against the back wall. There I stand in the twilight and close my eyes, feeling and hearing the wind against my auricles, willing it to carry muffled sounds and voices from somewhere distant: chatter in Irish, Yiddish, Italian and Polish, metal clashing on metal, blacksmiths competing in counterpoint.

∾

From the zone of industrial dereliction around Scotland Street to the reiterated Upperthorpe across the ring road, there once existed an uninterrupted mass of terraced streets and dilapidated back-to-backs. Obscured by acid smog, punctuated with airless courtyards and squalid middens, connected by back lanes and cobbled gennels.

The population was as concentrated as its dwellings: packed into foetid tenements, serviced by a frenetic commercial class of butchers, grocers, druggists and pawnbrokers, fuelled from a surfeit of public houses with alluring, lost identities: The Ball Inn, The Black Man, The Old Hussar, Farmyard Vaults, with Truswell's, Old Albion, Wards and Magnet on tap.

Immigrants came here because, like them, this place was at the bottom of the pile. Irishmen laid bricks for railways, steelworks and navigations. Italians carved marble and made terrazzo or mosaics. Catholic wed Catholic. New-generation citizens with exotic origins joined holy day processions down Solly Street.

From early on this melee of low-ranking humanity and hidden, unsanctioned activity was marked down as a threat to the ruling order. So on old maps we see outposts of surveillance and control – a grid of subjugation laid out over barbarian territory: churches, convents and chapels to harness souls; police stations, debtors' gaols and magistrates' courts to coerce and punish; boys' hostels, girls' institutes and Sunday Schools to redeem and reform. All committed to correcting the errant lives of drinkers, gamblers, brawlers and shaggers – seekers of spontaneous satisfaction, because the best they could hope for at the end of a short, hard life was a quick, painless death. But as with all imperial outposts, one suspects the occupiers, not the occupied, had their backs to the wall. Because the tangled thicket surrounding them was impenetrable, unconquerable.

The Ganglands

After the Great War this was a land unfit for heroes. With six thousand of their citizen comrades dead, the men who came back believed they had earned decent jobs and homes. Instead, they found poverty and the dole.

Output collapsed in the city's factories. The industry of death alone had excused high levels of production, employment and disposable income. In a country broke from war debt, austerity eroded municipal services. Poor relief cuts created a desperate underclass, seduced by gambling and its promise of instant redemption. A threadbare police force grappled with a spate of crime.

As impoverished as ever, this district descended further into dilapidation. All the pieces were in place for social breakdown: penury, bitterness and perceived betrayal, ineffective and disrespected institutions, a shattered urban landscape shrouding criminality.

The state has been defined by its monopoly on legitimate violence. But what happens when it fails? Living in peace isn't natural, it's a privilege of the protected. So the absence of government authority makes violence rational as well as feasible – a prerequisite for survival, the route to status and success.

Here, a band of local hoodlums filled the vacuum with a gamut of anti-social activities: card-sharping, extorting and pick-pocketing, assaulting publicans, pedestrians and taxi drivers, bleeding businesses dry with protection rackets. Then they strutted the city's streets like peacocks in flashy suits and ill-gotten gold watches.

Their leader was a liar, deserter and thug called Mooney – a man on the up from petty crime and spurious bookmaking. By 1918 he controlled the lucrative Sky Edge betting ring – beyond his home territory and high above the city, perfectly placed to spot and evade police raids. The game was simple and addictive: pitch and toss, with money staked on the fall of three coins. The business, in a long tradition of edgy enterprises, possessed its own peculiar lexicon, with pilners, ponters, towlers and tossers serving as sentries, enforcers, toll collectors and coin spinners, all reporting to the headman – Mooney himself.

While the city boomed and workers were flush with war wages, the ring turned a healthy profit. Mooney expanded the payroll beyond his core of West Bar cronies, recruiting men from the local Park district. But when the economy crashed and takings collapsed, he was quick to cut them loose. The Park men were bitter and out for revenge – a ready-formed rival gang. The joint was on their patch, after all.

What followed was a familiar gangland tale: rival factions fighting for control of space and a scarce, illicit revenue source, calibrated games of revenge and counter-revenge, tactical pauses and re-initiations, escalation and de-escalation. Victims were slashed or pummelled with razor blades, smashed bottles, pokers or iron chains. State institutions were corrupted by witness intimidation and soft sentences, handed down by bent officials. Violence was monopolised by reprobates. Perhaps inevitably the conflict crescendoed towards murder: a man beaten up with a child's scooter then stabbed in the stomach, bleeding out while his killers ate their fish and chips.

After three years of terror the episode ended with a robust reassertion of the state's remit. A police chief moulded in a brutal colonial force assembled a menagerie of hard men and war heroes: the twenty-stone ex-guardsman, the former heavyweight boxer, the man whose hands were so big they could each hold seven tennis balls. All drilled in self-defence by a continental jiu-jitsu champion.

Unconstrained by rules of engagement, this Flying Squad of bellicose oddballs met coshes and life preservers with boots, fists and regulation truncheons – wearing the gangsters down before finally finishing them off.

Renewal

Perhaps the institutions of officialdom share a collective memory, complete with grudges, refusing to forgive or forget the slights against them.

This patch of territory had shown it would never be brought to heel. Attempts to impose a matrix of domination had failed, deviance persisted between the citadels. Criminality, of course, but mostly the sins of autonomy and self-sufficiency in one-man enterprises – silent on St Mondays – and fortified extended families. A dangerous, competitor culture prevailed: spontaneous and insubordinate, too agile to trap, its codes beyond the outsider's grasp.

To its inhabitants this place was much more than the zone of shame marked on Corporation maps. It existed in their minds as an intricate mosaic – its luminous tesserae loaded with knowledge of values, meanings, traditions and terrains. Nooks and alleys beyond authority's reach, arcane modes of operation – fiddles, favours, tricks and techniques. A colourful cast of ale wives and wise women, nuns and nightsoil men, prize fighters and priests. Stories that endured in relics, stones, buildings and machines. A singular way of life described in a dialect of equal complexity. Indigenous expertise and the subversive authority it contained.

The cure would be extreme – removing the tumour completely.

Exponents of urban renewal were often driven by a worthy, reformist ambition – to transform the conditions of the poor. The slums were a disgrace – symbols of contempt for humble humanity. But razing neighbourhoods raises suspicions.

In the mid-twentieth century nearly everything here was flattened, along with three quarters of the city's old districts. (We used to think all those puddled car parks were legacies of the Blitz, but the Luftwaffe had nothing on this).

There seems to have been a lust to level, hidden behind the language of progress. In the city architect's own words, re-planning required the demolition of entire areas 'to their natural limits'. 'Fit' as well as 'unfit' houses would be condemned, sometimes in similar numbers. Something else was at work: an exercise in social reordering.

Among a profusion of motives and objectives – social improvement, moral redemption, authoritarian control, political advantage – one theme stands out: things being done to the powerless by the powerful. An elite of architects, surveyors, engineers, planners and councillors who knew they knew best and disdained inexpert opinion.

The city's re-creation was a declared exercise, or rather experiment, in rationalism – the dominant ideology of the age. Through the application of science and logic – to which these technocrats claimed exclusive access – uniform housing units would be machines for living, making resident minds more reasonable, shaping obedient lives of supervised work and rational leisure. Through Christian morality – with an agnostic makeover – sinners would be saved, their progress towards perfection recorded on the clipboards of embedded sociologists. And because there's no feeling quite like righteousness, it would all be done with urgency and evangelical zeal.

This part of town – between Upperthorpe and St Vincent's – became a showcase for the era's planning obsessions. A new ring road bisected the district, enabling rapid transport and the separation of people from traffic. *Rezoning* moved industry to the east of the road and housing to the west. Residents were relocated there – in high-rise towers and maisonettes – or dispersed to distant garden suburbs.

Viewed through a different lens these were actions straight from a user's guide to colonial domination: forced demolitions and resettlement, a district divided by a brutal, concrete barrier, a population kettled on the wrong side of the tracks. Destroying the city to save it. Today, this section of the Inner Ring Road has a solitary, oppressive underpass, with the road bearing down and walls that slope in. You could almost believe there was a 'plan' behind the planning, that the people here weren't really welcome in the new, gleaming, post-war city centre.

But what of the 'distilled' population? What did they think? The young, it seems, came off the best. Their nimble minds flexed to new realities, embracing the upsides of flushing toilets and sleek fitted kitchens. It was much harder for the old folk. In their minds the tesserae were fixed in place, the wisdom they contained too ancient to update. Detached from context, everything they knew was obsolete, even the names of things and turns of phrase. Some of them never got over it.

Studies said most of them were happy in their new situations. But moving was compulsory, going back, an impossibility. Acquiescence seems more likely. These were people who knew they lacked agency and understood how things worked. Experience told them the state can remove you at its whim – if not to the front then to the loony bin. In the mid-twentieth century fear of those places lived on in family discourse: 'Smarten yourself up or you'll end up in the Croft'.

Out at the city fringes, the Corporation garden estates took a gentler approach to remaking minds. By replicating middle-class settings – their designers' natural habitats – they would create a 'respectable working class.' This was a cohort my own family identified with, even while the phrase denigrated their origins.

Here, gardens and green space would civilise and tranquillise, while cleaner air soothed city-seared lungs. Pigeon-keeping, boozing and similar urban vices were banned or restricted. Revolutionary spirits would be quelled, by design or fortuitous side effect. We all know the cliché of the peasant with his pitchfork, but who ever revolted with a pair of privet hedge shears?

The Button Estate – at least in this outsider's childhood memories – was a setting for lives the garden city visionaries would have lauded. Leisure time was filled with green belt rambles, rose cuttings and clattering mowers. Husbands in tweed jackets and wives with blue rinses took pride in their respectability and relative status. But these were boys who had landed at Salerno and girls who had manned the munition factories. They had nothing more to prove. They had paid for their comfort and dignity.

~

Places exist in people's heads, where structures can be more stubborn than those in the physical world. So changing environments changed behaviour less than the social engineers might have hoped.

Rebuilt districts failed to build more rational minds. Influence flowed the other way, with citizens imposing their inherited, elaborate realities onto logical landscapes. Individuals bearing a city's cultural legacy failed to mutate into the flat inhabitants of architectural sketches. A way of life adapted, albeit diluted, and survived.

In defiance of meticulously laid plans, exuberant displays of bird boxes, feeders and ornamental kitsch violated minimalist lines. White goods awaiting removal, personal transportation devices, gas canisters and collections of pottery cats cluttered balconies intended for bistro tables.

Spaces conceived for approved activities adapted to casual uses: uncommodified and therefore dubious assemblies, informal enterprises run out of bedrooms and kitchens, recycled goods traded from lock-up garages – monetising materials wasted by legitimate others. Informal networks circumvented concrete barriers. Paths of convenience cut the corners off communal lawns. New, rich and vibrant mosaics were pieced together. Then the ultimate statement of individuality: mortgaged ownership and a personalised, Georgian-style front door – enough to give an architect hives.

After just a couple of decades, on estates across the city, the Corporation turned its back on experiments in radical social reordering. More demolition was followed by a new round of regeneration, applying the latest old-school philosophies.

This time neighbourhoods were rebuilt on a human scale, to look uncannily like their original versions: traditional constructions with pitched roofs clustered around intimate courtyards. For residents the experience might have been familiar – more things being done to them.

~

Back in the day, advocates of urban renewal shared a progressive assumption: that things would always get better. But now I stand here on Cross Smithfield peeling back the layers: of jerry-built, fifties industrial shacks, insanitary Victorian slums, mediaeval crofts and field forms, prehistoric strata of mudstone, siltstone and compacted sand, carrying their temporal cargoes of silver coins, animal bones and knife blanks. And topping it all – the most advanced iteration of this ever-changing landscape – the derelict expanses of post-progress, punctuated with towers of extractive student cubicles. Slums of the near future, surrounded by epoch-defining accumulations of rubbish.

Downfall

Cities, at the hands of analysts and statisticians, are endlessly evaluated, measured and compared – their levels of output, income and investment, their prosperity and productivity, their indices of multiple deprivation. And this one can be trusted to appear in the lowest quartile of any given ranking – because the reason it came to be is no longer reason to exist.

At its peak the city was a tightly woven fabric – of in-the-know networks, value chain linkages, circular relationships and precarious dependencies – all built on a base of carbon. In satellite villages with no other industries, armies of miners hewed coal from the ground, coking plants turned the coal into potent fuel for the city's furnaces, then the furnaces made steel so the workshops could make everything else – battleships, turbines, steam locomotives – all powered by coal.

But depleted seams, inflated costs and cleaner alternatives sealed King Coal's fate. And when the threads of the carbon economy failed the entire construction fell to pieces.

In the factories, overcapacity and ancient machinery produced inevitable results – lines of red numbers in company ledgers. Complacent managers and owners drank whisky from lunchtime and splurged profits on Rollers and Rovers – abstaining only from innovation and investment. Workers' syndicates resisted automation and modern practices, their centuries-old collective memory reminding them that compromise precedes obsolescence.

But downfall, in the end, was caused by a purposeful act of destruction, shabbily disguised as self-correcting market forces. Labour unity was countered with a vicious strain of monetarism, unleashing chain reactions of debt defaults, bankruptcies and mass redundancies. Factories were closed down then asset-stripped, their machinery flogged to post-colonial upstarts. Roofs were removed to dodge property taxes, then the walls were demolished. The industrial heartland turned into a wasteland, like the aftermath of area bombing.

Like Carthage (another place once made rich from metals production) imperial forces sacked the city and salted its earth – the generals, this time, in tailored suits, their foot soldiers in police uniforms. In the melee the great economist was murdered, his corpse desecrated. Micro-profit triumphed over macro-prosperity – comeuppance for centuries of impudence.

But in truth, decline had set in years before. This place, like the Empire that once nourished it, peaked more than a century and a half ago. Like Timbuktu and Petra the trade routes shifted, the world economy relocated, the city moved from centre to sleepy periphery.

And now we dwell here in the ruins of a fallen civilisation, crouching in these valleys under low, gloomy skies, our heads bowed, chippy from reduced circumstances, insular and parochial. The city's a failure based on multiple metrics, with recovery always around the next blind corner.

The River – Part Three

At the toll bar roundabout the river guards a crescent of alms houses – ideal cottages for exhibits of the worthy poor. High gables, imposing chimney stacks, end walls with diamonds of clinker bricks – puritan charity announced on a prominent datestone. Soul salvation for all.

A culvert guides the river under the road, into a canyon dividing boozers from evangelicals, supervised by a fat, damp rat squatting on a capstone. King of this territory, with his own can of Super and a half-eaten saveloy.

The gully cuts through a monoculture of terraced houses: river-view yards colourised with lavender, blue bins and red roses, high boundary walls for protection from muroids and leptospirosis.

The valley road's a repository of memories: the lonely wife in a frosted chip shop window, the medicine shop where girls proffered happiness in upstairs rooms, the dealer waxing nostalgic in his wax jacket – a conga line and bunting at the end of the war.

He narrates the pub's permutations down the years: students in black in the back, wasters in the tap room planning boiler heists from neighbouring houses. Now it's some kind of wine bar where a kid checks your booking on a tablet. A couple strolled in there with gold Rolexes, popped collars and silk neck scarves.

'Christ, they looked like they'd stepped off a bloody yacht.'

The Self-rulers

So that's that. The city's a failure. But there's another side to this story for us to ponder. Because most people here seem to be more or less … what? Happy? Too much. Contented, at least.

The growth doctors prescribe more big corporates, more GDP. But no one here seems desperate to enlist in the black polyester armies that scuttle the streets of more affluent cities – clutching frappuccinos with plastic lids and depleted tubes of cold sore cream, fulfilling other people's Missions in performative team meetings.

Because at its heart this is a city of self-rulers and freelancers – descendents of stubbornly autonomous artisans with their own backyard smithies. Simultaneously entrepreneurs and contract labourers, working alone or placing outwork as needed, toiling while disdaining the work-religion, packing it up when enough's been done, taking time off for fishing or St Monday down at the pub.

Strangers to capital, these *individuals* shared a precarity that shaped common values, and a counter-intuitive collective identity. Robustly self-reliant, they looked out for each other, through unions, mutual aid and quiet acts of charity. And they stood together in the face of power and money – maestro and apprentice, a team united in craft and sweat, not master and servant divided by profit.

Today's self-rulers take a variety of intriguing forms. Small business owners commit the cardinal sin of 'lifestyling' – slowing down or kicking back when there's enough in the bank, not pushing on to earn, own and display more. Grant-funded growth advisers face walls of resistance when they advocate getting serious – business planning, investor propositioning, leveraging, profit maximising. Following other people's rules.

Others lead lives of richly textured enterprise in defiance of capital's diktats: blending paid labour – enough to get by – with simple pleasures and acts of generosity, hustling, but for fun as much as money, flogging antiques or old clothes, relishing the social life of the car boot. Employment is irregular hours baking cakes, stripping doors, cleaning houses or on the tills, all mixed up with errands for old ladies, dealing with the kids, helping out at school.

Some take fierce pride in fiscal self-reliance – for them autonomy means never taking a penny from anyone. Others are virtuoso freeloaders, inheritance parasites or benefits wanglers – because freedom's never so sweet as when the government foots the bill (and besides, an ancient class-consciousness tells them the rich are the biggest freeloaders of all). Self-rule is a cross-cutting category, intersecting the virtues and vices of bourgeois morality.

Some see owning property as a route to autonomy (with equity growth creating time-limited opportunities to live well without graft). Others prefer to rent, viewing the mortgage and its bastard child – home maintenance – as the primary instruments of vassalage (a sentimental hangover, perhaps, from the glory days of social housing, when enriching hobbies could be pursued at the kitchen table while the man from the council wrestled with the plumbing). When you're skint, which you will be, self-rule demands compromise.

And all of this is loosely interspersed, whenever the feeling takes us, with meandering dog walks, funny chats with strangers in the street or on the bus, drives out to the dams, urban exploration, duck contemplation.

Self-rule, therefore, comes in many guises, but with the same essential characteristics: living less quickly, savouring the world's unenclosed pleasures, forfeiting the deadly sins of pride, greed and envy (if not sloth). These are the joys and rewards, unmentionable in these puritanical times, of simply tossing it off.

All of which forces us to challenge the technocrat's negative appraisal, the endless quest for regeneration, transformation and expansion. This place won't change because no one here wants it to. Too much would be lost. And we certainly aren't going to sweat for it.

This isn't failure, only the rejection of a suspect, alien notion of success. But it could be a template for what comes next – a blueprint for contentment after the final crash, after we've extracted too much from the earth.

The Monkey Puzzle Tree

Changed into his pyjamas, ready for bed, the boy has squeezed himself into the gap between the sash window – open, just a crack – and the drop-leaf table – decorated with a doily and flowers in a glass vase. The fading summer day broadcasts its amplified hum. An old couple stroll back from the Horticultural Society – a tweed jacket with a regimental tie, a light-blue cardi she knitted herself. The Sailor's Ford Escort squats by the grass verge – police blue with a black vinyl roof.

These are the things that busy his senses. But only one object fascinates: the tree almost obscuring the house across the road, one you could twist into existence with a packet of green and brown pipe cleaners. Is the monkey hiding in there somewhere? Do all those spikes and curling branches hold the answer to his puzzle?

In the living room's grey, powdery light, the Matriarch returned from the kitchen with two mugs of what she only ever called a 'hot milk drink' – the Stores' answer to Horlicks, I think. Mimicking the gait of Mammy Two Shoes in tan stockings and slippers, making us giggle:

'Tho-mas! … Tho-mas!'

The Valor gas fire filled the room with sticky warmth. The home-stitched snake with the funny face stymied its escape under the door. Morecambe and Wise, in big bow ties, showed off to their glamorous guest star. On the coffee table the Mercer was going nowhere – screwed to the black ashtray, missing its driver's seat.

The thirties sideboard, its curves carved with swirls and flowers, displayed souvenirs of the Sailor's travels: a pair of Chinese immortals with staffs and flowing robes, the ship's crest mounted on a shield of salvaged hardwood – Comus with his lascivious mouth, masticating memories of moonlight encounters.

When I tired of the scene outside, I crossed the room to sit on the Sailor's knee – in the swivel chair and the glow of the standard lamp, beneath the framed print of sailing ships on the Medway at dusk. Snuggling with this big, gentle man. Trying hard not to be irritating – he lacked experience with children and could get a little testy.

The shelves beside him sagged with books on his favourite, nostalgic subjects: all the warships that ever displayed the city's name and shining bell, the rivers of the west side and their lost water mills (7/6 scribbled on a brown paper cover – a price as mysterious as hieroglyphics), the flood that laid waste to the valley (grainy daguerreotypes of men with broken machines, in a frayed, orange sleeve). Beside his chair a magazine rack groaned with fading copies of the *Navy News*.

He had a gift for drawing – one of many honed during long ocean voyages. So with a pencil stub and pad he delighted me with sketches of BSA motorbikes and sleek, mid-century sports cars. Now the night was falling outside and the curtains were drawn. The room induced a valerian drowse – the viscous, balmy air; soft bodies and silent affection; the hollow tock of the grandmother clock, imposing her endless rhythm on the silence.

For this young boy, he was the most satisfying of old seafarers: a beard abundant enough to pass without prosthesis at school Christmas parties; thick, hairy forearms; the ideal navy tattoo – a white ensign wrapped around a blurry blue anchor. I wondered if he noticed my eyes on him, scrutinising every detail. The way his hands moved slowly, selecting a sheet of gummed paper and a pinch of Old Holborn, rolling a slender cigarette between thumb and middle finger, distributing the tobacco with a nimble forefinger from above. Was he conscious of my microscope focused on the clumps of hair that sprouted from his ears, the miniature rivers of dilated blood vessels in his nose? And, most curious of all, the fossilised accumulation beneath his thumbnail – the consequence, perhaps, of a mishap in a garden shed or motor workshop.

During the afternoon we might have sat in the garden, on orange cushions on the bench by the back door, glugging lemonade while the adults drank tea and completed the crossword (resorting to *Pears Cyclopedia* for the final word). This was grown-up territory, not a place for children to play, with precision-pruned roses and sacred lawn edges, the grass as weedless and uniform as the bowling greens down in the park.

At the end of the garden, beyond the bean frames, the shed and the greenhouse, a steep grass bank rose to a place I was eager to explore but knew to be forbidden. The Sailor said there was a reservoir up there but I thought he was fibbing. I'd seen it from Ben Lane when I'd walked along the wall, balancing on the curved cap stones – just a flat expanse of grass interrupted by concrete squares, a board game for giants. He chuckled and tried to explain. The reservoir was underneath, he said, in a chamber as big as a football pitch with a roof over the top. From that day I dreamed of dinghies with white sails tacking in an endless nighttime, illuminated by a crescent moon swinging from a ceiling painted the deepest blue, with twinkling spotlights standing in for stars.

The Sailor might have driven us out to the country on the city's north side – to Wortley or Whitley or one of those places – to meet a man in blackened overalls with a traction engine parked in a field, for a chat in a lost language about levers and boilers and fettling spare parts. And on the way home he might have pulled the Escort over to the side of a country lane, taken his spade from the boot and shovelled horse manure off the road into hessian sacks. For the roses, a nutritious godsend.

At bedtime we climbed the stairs to our room where the double bed was made with shiny, crimson sheets. (There was little else in there, just a dressing table and a small, oak wardrobe – a museum exhibit of a time before people filled their houses with things).

Mum had told us that she'd shared that same big bed with her two sisters. To get to sleep they'd played a game: tracing shapes with forefingers on each other's backs – the recipient guessing what the picture might be. I lay there with my brother and we did the same. It was comforting in that familiar, unfamiliar place, filled with obsolete objects, smells and textures. Not unpleasant but as different as a foreign country. A remnant of a lost age.

Dreamfields

At the city's southern border, the territorial struggle between ancient kingdoms and their successors has carried on for millennia. Almost twelve hundred years ago, in a village whose name meant *gateway*, the King of Wessex and Mercia (that is, of all the bloody southerners) received the submission of the King of Northumbria (and with him all the bloody northerners). Only recently absorbed within the city's expanded boundaries, the village now celebrates the conquering monarch – treacherously? – in the name of its school. At the fringe of an unassuming and stubbornly proletarian metropolis, this is a place of questionable provenance: of businessmen in pink polo shirts and Doric-columned mansions, high-end osteopaths and lash beauticians, ladies in gold Rolexes and red lipstick lunching at the Caffè d'Amour, upscale architects touting glass boxes to WAGs and their wing backs.

More recently the tables have turned, with the city on aggressive manoeuvres for more than a century. From the old border line of the Limb and Meers brooks (the names of both meant *division*), slices of the county to the south have been targeted, harassed and annexed to accommodate massive overspill populations.

In a never-ending war of attrition the front line has shifted by just a couple of miles, the conquered territories consolidated with facts on the ground. Vast, sub-Corbusier estates of flats and maisonettes have risen on pretty countryside fringing prosperous, privet hedge suburbs. A socialist Corporation kicking the petty bourgeoisie where it hurts – right in the house prices. Inevitably the city's neighbours have grown prickly and paranoid, on one occasion comparing a post-war act of 'territorial brigandage' to Hitler's quest for lebensraum.

Beyond one of the city's system-built urban transplants, nestled in a wide, shallow valley and protected precariously by a no man's land just three fields wide in places (no territorial three-mile limit here) is the place that formed me.

The city bears down on this satellite town like the dark mass of Anatolia over a Dodecanese island. Its inhabitants clad themselves in metaphorical Kevlar to man bureaucratic green-belt barricades, or instigate resistance campaigns in defence of their Midlands postal identity. But the city's influence is irrepressible, flowing over the border in commuter traffic, football allegiances, and the defiled tributary that feeds the River Drone from its city-side source.

When it was built this was supposedly the continent's largest private housing estate, a fact residents would once remind you of with a curious pride and special stress on the word *private*. Across the valley uniform boxes were laid out for miles, as though planned by a child of stifled imagination supplied with a box of identical Danish plastic bricks. In every one of them, mortar crumbles between reconstituted stone – concrete cancer for the owner-occupier classes, a legacy of too much sand in the mix.

So what was it that attracted my parents' generation here – to this artificial island of purpose-built pubs and five-shop precincts, miles from anywhere, hooking them on cars like crystal meth? To understand, you have to turn the clock back to the time just before my birth.

This was the age of the Ideal Home, when the charm of the city's Victorian terraces and thirties semis was yet to be rediscovered. For now, especially if you'd been dragged up in them, your monochrome memories were of soot-soiled chimney stacks, death-hazard three-bar fires and a freezing privy outside the back door. This, in brilliant colour contrast, was Dreamfields, a new world of off-road carports and perpetually warm radiators, where you could have a cat and actually swing it in the third bedroom. Then there was the clincher: you paid lower rates for all this privilege. Objectively, nothing was not to like. To employ the estate agent's cliché, it ticked all the boxes. To move to Dreamfields was to reject the past and the antiquated, at a time when both deserved rejection.

This was a settlement focused entirely on future possibilities, symbolising an age of opportunity and frenetic physical and social mobility (with good motorway connections for the going-places commercial traveller). The city had kept their parents in their places, from birth to slow-then-sudden death by industrial diseases. But for this unbounded generation of yes-sayers moving here would be their act of unburdening, of history and memory erasure, of throwing off the chains of low expectations. In their modern, light-filled homes, more space enabled manic levels of consumption and object accumulation, diarrhetic gift exchanging and gadget buying. Gluttony to remedy post-war starvation. Cars were replaced and upgraded with dizzying frequency, engine spec and number plate giveaways noted in unspoken neighbourly knockouts. Luxury caravans were crammed into driveways, equity released and recycled into endlessly evolving extensions.

Pastimes were traditional, deferential, and usually organised in this best of all possible worlds. Light opera am-dram, gang shows and harvest festivals. Children in quasi-military uniforms saluting flags, the Queen and the Almighty in God-aligned prefab huts. Sport was compulsory, introspection frowned upon. Moving too fast. Always moving up.

Tales of naughtiness circulated in whispers: vicars and tarts, car keys in ashtrays, cheeky wife swaps. All revealing the fundamental paradox: these were the grandchildren of buttoned-up Victorians and the feral progeny of the sexual revolution – impossible opposites reconciled in individual bodies (and in the odd swinging couple). Shut the kids in the bedroom and party, because you've never had it so good!

With time, relative isolation and the paucity of distractions gave rise to an impressive talent for inventing entertainments – a cultural microclimate that puts the city's repressed render and red-brick suburbs to shame. Galas are packed with pyroartists, pedagogic first aiders, ladies' choirs and unicorn pony rides. Arts festivals advertise jiu-jitsu workshops, lockdown-vintage baptist ukulele groups, belrobics and hula hoop instruction. Women are watched knitting with giant balls of wool.

Viewed from outer space the town is revealed as a phoenix – the sprawling estates to the east and west her flaming wings, the parallel lines of the bypass and the old main road her extended neck, the roundabout with the carboot and the carvery her unblinking eye, the dual carriageway slicing through the council estates her long, narrow beak, snacking on the city from beneath.

This was my parents dream and they lived it well, through long barbecue nights in summer and weightless New Year's parties, dancing to Boney M with the furniture moved to the edges of the room. Perhaps inevitably it wasn't mine. I went in search of something different, just as they had turned their backs on their parents' world. But trying to understand why has been a journey of revelation, burrowing into the bedrock of my identity. At first, I explained it as a quest for texture and patina – the meaning that accumulates in old things. From a young age I was absorbed by what lay beneath the new town's physical monoculture: the remains of bell pits and spoil heaps in the woods near our house, the ivy-covered ruins of an old cottage in the field beyond the estate, the rusted VW with flaking turquoise paint, dumped in a disused quarry. Anything old found in the ground. Things from the time before the world was straightened out. Before the crooked roads of genius were bulldozed for the bypass.

Where reality was threadbare, I would imagine wondrous concealed things: relics, ideally from the war, in the locked up hut I found in the woods or an abandoned factory in the town's old centre. But nourishment was hard to find in the wasteland. One day I stood at the top of our road and experienced something like a vision. As I looked on, the new houses that rose up the hillside collapsed into heaps of rubble, shaken to pieces by a powerful, rolling earthquake. I was satisfied. The obsession was to obliterate the new, to go back, to descend into the past, to be consumed by it. The disease, it seemed, was a strange kind of nostalgia – for an age before my birth, an alluring but necessarily unreal, imagined world.

As an adult, the disease drew me here, to live in the old city, first in terraced houses inhabited by friendly ghosts, now in a centenarian semi scratched with the chisel marks of long-passed craftsmen, autographed with the builder's crest in a luminescent stained-glass window. Faced with a paucity of valuable minerals on the surface, the miner digs deeper, searching for richer treasures, scouring the broken remains of the once-virile metropolis, obsessing over signs in stones and fractures in landscapes. Unearthing the bones of ancestors he restores them to life, surprising himself with the acute pain and comfort of their presence. An exposed wound soothed with a calendula balm. The city swallows him up, itself becoming the illness.

But weird nostalgia only begs the question: what in turn is the nostalgia's root cause? Through mental excavations I find the answer in the date of my birth, or rather, further back, in the Big Bang, the very moment of creation. That fateful encounter between Dad's ebullient seed and Mum's wholesome ovum coincided precisely with the miners' strike and power station shutdowns of February 1972 – events that marked the end of the post-war party. My parents explained my existence with good humour and their essential chirpy optimism:

'The lights were out. It was cold. What else were we supposed to do?'

Nostalgia, it transpires, is only the symptom. The disease is something different. The diagnosis is declinism. I am decline's miserable offspring. Degeneration is intrinsic to my being, the cause of my melancholy. This isn't borne out in statistics or material facts, of course. My childhood was far more comfortable than those of my parents. You could say it's all a trick of the mind. But trajectory is everything. In spite of relative poverty, their world had been on the up. With all the metrics showing improvement there can still be malaise of the spirit.

Decline was everywhere during my formative years: the inevitable nightly announcements of factory closures and massed redundancies on the evening news, the expanses of steelworks in the city's East End suddenly transformed into deserts of rubble. We were sheltered on our island, no doubt, but harsh winds blew in from the world beyond, carrying the whiff of pestilence. In 1984, when miners' wives asked for tins at our local supermarket, they were looked down on, like paupers from the other side of a wall. And there were sniggers when the strike leader, in accented English only a degree broader than our own, said a policeman had hit him on the head. But we were all taking blows to the head and the body too. This, it would gradually become clear, was an assault on all of us.

Those were momentous times, possibly of millennial significance. The final stage of a Spenglerian cycle. Through the Ladybird books on my shelves and my mother's unswerving belief in forward momentum – the doctrine of progress – I had constructed a comforting world of order and stability: of overalled men bringing bags of coal on their lorries and shoulders, of smiling grown-ups in respected, perfectly painted roles: the bus driver, the fireman, the nurse, the gas board engineer. These were the contented but endangered inhabitants of the corporate state and the Button Estate, where the Matriarch still lived and Mum had grown up.

The real world around us was fracturing and subsiding, its assets stripped, its reassuring certainties subject to hostile takeover. There were no smiling coalmen here. Communities were eroding into losers and disconnected individuals, society attacking itself like a broken immune system. The old folk just looked on, lost and confused. The order and progress had, of course, all been in my mind. But six hundred years had passed, with a sustained upward trend line, since Chaucer's reeve had borne in his hose a thwitel of this city. From this moment on the curve would fall. The knife, most likely, would be made in China.

Which explains why, when I want to feel comfort, I close my eyes and take myself back to that front room at Hallowmoor, with the monkey puzzle tree and a hot milk drink, the Sailor and the Matriarch. Everything was just right then, slow and unchanging, in my imagined city. At other times I close my eyes and dream of leaving – for a New World with vast, cloudless skies and a long, straight road that never ends. Cleansed of memory. My own Dreamfields.

Pilgrims

The matchday ritual stretches back three generations (before that, on my grandfather's side at least, they were Baggies – economic migrants from a different metal-bashing city). The same assembly point – a pint at the Top House, the same (downhill) peregrination – like Canterbury, Aachen or Santiago. The same quest for redemption through communion with the divine.

In the arena, below the gable and the imperial box, the players emerge in glorious vertical stripes. Bright white lights, rock music testing the tannoy, meat extract incense. Emotion-rousing ruses as old as Rome, witnessed at the Colosseum, honed to perfection over centuries by the true church. Feelings ascend from the deep strata – vibrations in the torso, rising up through the chest and the neck, moisture on the eyeballs (is it only me?).

Memories embellished. A seven-year-old boy with his dad and a new scarf. A precision pass forward from the left, bisecting the defence. TC – Charles II perm, magnificent moustache – strolls it round the keeper, traps the ball on the goal line, pauses to punch the air then nonchalantly taps it in. Except it never happened quite like that, or perhaps it did in a different game on a different day. Like a child's perfect recall of a chat with the Virgin Mary.

A hunch-backed Spion Kop. A skinny lad and his mates leaning on blue barriers with two-pound tickets and ten packs of Silk Cut. Older blokes with brown leather jackets and Hamlet cigars. Ray and uncle Dick strolling down to the ground back in the fifties. I was sure I could hear the drum roll of feet on the old wooden floor.

Digging deeper. Cricketers kicking a ball to stay in shape through the winter, assembling a team for midweek evenings. Rules thrashed out at the Adelphi Hotel – free kicks, throw-ins and handballs. The mob game at Bents Green in the year Robespierre met Madame Guillotine – masses of men clashing over three days. Casualties, of course, but surprisingly no lives lost.

After the game we hiked back up the hill to the Matriarch's house – passing Victorian villas, Button Estate semis and the Sundial Club, where they met years before at the dance. Inexpert analysis – firmly held opinions, grades of shade and sunshine. Navigating heaven or hell to the house at the top with the alluring golden glow.

Entering the warmth: a wall lined with watercolours of the lost village (by the Major – one of her admirers), the Matriarch and the Sailor waiting upstairs on oak, thirties dining chairs. Scores and match reports on the radio – the wireless. I sat in the corner in his mother's Windsor chair, but I could no longer fit my finger into the hole in the paddle of its arm.

A clatter at the front door – instant reportage, almost magical, on green newsprint still warm from the press. We check the pools for score draws and thaw our insides with strong tea from the Stores. The Matriarch moves fluidly from fridge to counter top: a knife with two blades, breadcakes spread with marge, loaded with pickle and pressed tongue.

Christmas Day

The Sailor died on Christmas Day in the evening. At sixty-three he was too young. At fifteen, so was I. The cause of death was a second heart attack and before that, I suspect, too many years of processed rations, navy scran, and breakfasts fried in pig fat. Typically, for a man of his generation and class, a multitude of poisons probably also contributed – decades of high-tar cigarettes, polluted air and hazardous materials in ships and workshops, an early-fifties port stop in Hiroshima, oblivious to the dangers.

In the morning, the women had been in the kitchen downstairs, preparing the turkey with all the roast trimmings. (On Boxing Day, the Sailor would take the bird's remains to create his legendary, annual turkey curry). The men and boys – Dad, the Sailor, my brother and I – were upstairs in the living room. (The house really was laid out like that. A few years before they'd moved from the Button Estate to a new home in the village – further up the hill, split level and upside down from being built into the hillside, but still reassuringly familiar, with the same old objects and furniture).

There, with the winter sun streaming in and a clear view over the city to the east and south – Parkwood Springs, town, the tips of Netherthorpe towers – we gathered around him as he blew carols on his old Hohner harmonica, his eyes and cheeks beaming above his full, grey beard. Turn the scenery, switch to monochrome, change location. We could have been ratings huddled among the hammocks in the metallic belly of the Comus, somewhere in the East China Sea on a lost December morning.

He was born in the late twenties, the son of a Boer War veteran. In the last war he was too young to see action, enlisting with the Home Guard instead. His older brother served as a rear gunner in a Lancaster bomber – one of the war's most perilous and revered occupations. For a committed son of Empire there was much to live up to, but I suspect his love of sailing, nurtured on the dams of the city's north-west fringes, steered him towards a career in the navy.

From the late forties to the late fifties he served as an able seaman, mostly on the destroyer Comus, in the Far East. The incidents he described were vignettes of the Empire's dying days and the nascent Cold War: an attack by Ilyushins in the Yellow Sea, at the start of the Korean conflict, bombarding communist insurgents ensconced in jungles on the Malayan coast.

Other stories were imbued with his endearing, gentle humour. On shore leave one time, in Hong Kong, he was waylaid by one of his daft capers or esoteric quests (he wasn't the boozing or womanising sort). So he arrived late to the designated jetty, missing the last motor launch back to the ship, moored offshore in the harbour.

With his usual ingenuity and honourable intentions, he found a solution – to 'borrow' a little rowing boat from a sheltered corner of the harbour, where parents with young children rented them out by the hour. With his strong arms and sailor's competence, I imagine him powering a pair of tiny oars across moonlit water – a whiskery sea dog commanding a five-foot vessel with a silly duck's head and painted plumage.

Unfortunately, when he pulled alongside the steel wall of the Comus's hull, there was no chance of sneaking aboard. He was promptly arrested for going AWOL – a misdemeanour aggravated by suspected ship theft. He described pleading his innocence without much conviction, and an unconvincing dressing down by a ship's captain who clearly liked him and no doubt found the situation humorous. But it made no difference. He still spent that night as a prisoner in the ship's brig.

After demobilising, and for most of the sixties, he seems to have lived an old-fashioned bachelor's life – repairing lorries, and probably everything else, in the workshop of a refractory brick factory, sailing his dingy on Damflask at weekends, building a boundless variety of machines, models and contraptions – locomotives, lathes and water mills – some of which he actually finished.

The most impressive and eccentric was the Kan-Tiki – a raft named in honour of a famous vessel with a similar name that crossed the Pacific in the 1940s, itself replicating the imagined journey of a fanciful, sun-worshipping, Aryan tribe. His was assembled from repurposed planks, ropes and oil cans, then sailed on the choppy waters of a great estuary, dodging between massive tankers and cargo ships. The expedition was generally considered to be as mad as the one it emulated, carrying a significant risk of the Sailor killing himself.

He met the Matriarch in the late sixties, through a dancing class at the Sundial Club. Her first love and first husband had died prematurely some years earlier, and she'd raised her four children on her own. I suspect her affection for the Sailor was something different – love on a lower heat, the kind that thrives in a Mark-2 Escort's front seats, with gentle words and a ham sandwich picnic, watching the sea at Sandsend.

In my world, that Christmas Day wasn't how it should have been. It was a stupid kid's thing. The night before, with my parents out and a gang of friends in the house, we'd spilt red wine on the white living room carpet – ruining it. Dad, from whom the bottle had no doubt been liberated, was, shall we say, unimpressed.

On Christmas morning I was still sulking from the shame and the rollocking, not to mention a thumping headache. I wish it hadn't been that Christmas Eve. Why did it have to be red? And white for that matter? The carpet was replaced long ago but the mark has never gone away.

And there was something else – a serpent raising its head. This was an age at which the pieces of the adult world were starting to fall into place, the simple stories of childhood unveiling their complicated truths. I'd always known the Sailor wasn't my real grandfather, but it had never concerned me. Now this knowledge was lodged at the forefront of my thoughts. Old enough to comprehend, too childish to deal with it. The fact of our unrelatedness became a heavy cloud, looming over the time we spent together, constantly visible to me and I suspect to him too, because he saw it reflected my eyes.

My world was already transforming but it changed forever that day, halfway through Del Boy and Rodney. An ambulance came and took the Sailor away. The Matriarch, Dad and my brother went with him. They decided I was too young – a sound judgement, really. Later a call came from the hospital to tell us he'd died. I fell into Mum's lap and cried loudly. It wasn't authentic. Still incompletely formed, with no experience of bereavement, I didn't know that grief bides its time. I did what I thought people did, displaying emotions you had to feel.

I'm sure Mum knew it was an act. The guilt still lingers. Since that day I've imagined the Sailor watching over me, with pure affection stained by disappointment.

The pain of loss is something we bury, fearing how we'll feel if we scratch away at the back-filled ground. Recently I've excavated my memories, visiting the Sailor's places, searching for traces, seeking to recover pure experiences unsullied by knowledge.

I remember how I felt when I sat on his knee, entranced as frigates and motorbikes flowed from the tip of his pencil, carried away over distant, exotic seas, in awe of that perfect mariner's mark – the blue anchor and ensign on his forearm. There was distance, of course – this was a son of Victorians. But most of all I remember his gentleness, softness and physical warmth, wrapping itself around me.

I think of him often, with deep affection, and sadness that we could never speak man to man, connecting with clear eyes and innocent smiles.

The River – Part Four

The river flows past the mid-terrace where me and my old mate – flat cap on indoors, tilted with precision – slouched in the living room. Foraged sixties sofa, bile-style carpet, rolling Drum and necking booze-cruise wine into the early hours.

Boxes of contraband stacked in corners – for sale or immediate consumption, faulty gas fire pilfering oxygen. Light-headed know-alls losing the plot – bizarre business plans, addled politics, gripes and tall tales.

Fetching the next bottle from the five-pound fridge with the death rattle – cooled to imperfection with a bag of river trout and a tub of turmeric maggots.

The Board Meeting

In the tool company boardroom the thud of the drop forge was dull but unremitting. Patinated panels vibrated on the walls. Technologies from a different century gathered dust on a flaking, hand-painted exhibition board – wooden-handled adzes, gouges and tenon saws.

Three generations held their positions around the immovable oak table, its scuffed leather surface laid with Empire cutlery for fish luncheon – an old Friday tradition. Dear Mrs Bayliss would be serving them soon.

The hammer maintained its rhythm.

In the senior seat, Young George – navy tie with a v-neck sweater, heavy rimmed glasses for high myopia – maintained a barrier of firmly folded arms. Without a word, the latest proposal had been overruled. The board meeting minutes would tell the story of how the decision had been reached:

The managing director (a constipated sexagenarian) presented the facts. Foreign competitors were thrashing them on price and features. Moulded plastic handles – competitive edge. With the forge failing and the dies worn out all their famous brand could promise was dubious quality at premium prices. The bank account was depleted, the workforce superannuated. They had to take action!

Giles, a property consultant and one-time school friend, had appraised the building and seen potential. Admittedly, the hill's gradient and unsuitability for goods vehicles made industrial uses unviable. But industry was history, Giles said. The future was in education – forging the minds of new generations. And towers of en-suites with shared social spaces were a booming asset class.

Detailed plans and sketches were presented on a new-fangled device – brick-effect blocks squeezed onto an awkward polygon, foreign student cutouts carrying bags and books. Industry in absentia. The youngest director made cautious, supporting forays, followed swiftly by withdrawal to the safety of defensive positions.

The project would be transformational, the managing director said. A huge cash payment or eternal rents from a fourteen-storey golden goose. That could fund a modern factory, product innovation, the company's rebirth.

Perhaps because of his visual impairment it took the chairman some time to realise that the proposed edifice would rise precisely where he was seated. This shrine where mythical deals had been sealed, the patent screwdriver's church of conception, Old George's cracked-leather chair. A blueprint for demolition. Memory's obliteration.

Silence. Folded arms. And then:

'Thank you, son. I think it's time for luncheon, don't you?'

The managing director's head returned to its customary bowed position, his humbled eyes drawn to a familiar, barely visible mark in the leather table top, created years before by the wheels of one of his toy vehicles. For now he would carry on with his worthy local endeavours – honorary this, deputy that, president of some obscure entity or other, upholder of precarious status and arcane tradition. And the young man would move away to fulfil the duty of his regimental commission, before coming back. To wait, and wait…

The Empty Chair

Old Mary was there, sitting to attention in her armchair. Bands of sunlight streamed in through the bay window, settling on the flattened curls of her white hair. Her eyes, narrowed to stiletto blades, were trained on the viewers in the hallway, scrutinised through the glass in the living room door.

On the table beside her an old silver Walkman groaned. The delicate notes of a piano concerto trickled from the cushions of her headphones. In her lap skilled fingers moved instinctively, needles clicking together with unconscious precision. Knit two, knit two together, knit four. A cardigan for little Paul, her latest great-grandchild.

She had no wish to hear any more from these people – the oily estate agent apologising for her and Paweł's things, yet another young couple talking indiscreetly about removing walls, stripping back plaster, starting with a clean state. The pair gawped through the glass door panel, grinning like eejits at a collection of curiosities that might have been curated by aliens: a peaked rogatywka on an oak fifties sideboard, emblazoned with a polished, crowned eagle, an oil painting on the wall in dull mid-century tones – a young cavalry officer on horseback in a forest glade, wearing the same four-cornered cap, a portrait of John Paul II in white cassock and zucchetto, bathed in rays of holy light. A black and white photograph showed a bride and groom outside a church with a belfry that didn't quite fit, her face a pristine window onto unblemished joy, his betraying his burden – the knowledge that treasures can be lost in a moment.

And they saw two identical armchairs, one empty, and one occupied by the frail old woman who didn't seem all there. Over the years she'd changed their fabrics as fashions came and went – atomic, then geometric, then floral. Now they were a practical beige on which she hadn't even been consulted. No bother; at least her rule had been followed – the two had to be the same.

For those who knew their necessary order, the piles of books on the shelves by the chimney breast told the story of an extraordinary journey. Through modern-day Ukraine, Romania, Hungary and Croatia, to France and the north-eastern fringes of the island that would become the wanderer's final home.

It was only in the late nineteen seventies, after three decades had passed, that the book collecting started and Paweł began to talk. But even then it was only of a fantastical odyssey – reality remade as a boy's adventure story: the return to his parents' flat in Lwów and an urgent civilian transformation, the melee of a government office where papers were stamped with haste and shared out like pączki, chaotic rides to the Romanian Bridgehead in peasants' carts and geriatric armoured cars – recounted with dashes of slapstick. A freezing Carpathian crossing became an invigorating Scout hike, a shambolic breakout from an insecure internment camp an exemplar of officer panache.

Paweł described murmurating masses of refugees at Budapest's Kelenföld station, then a furtive train trip to the border town of Barcs for a cinematic, moonlit crossing of the Drava River. The final scene twisted through the hills and forests of Yugoslavia, to the port of Split and the crowded steamer that would carry him to Marseille – where the battalion of a city still unknown to him had stepped ashore a quarter of a century earlier.

In France he would rejoin his country's army, once again fighting a rearguard action against invasion before a final retreat across the Channel. Most of all he enjoyed recounting idyllic years spent in Scotland, defending the Lothian coast against an unlikely invasion (Mary suspected he had a girl up there but never asked). That was until 1944, when his historical record became obscure once again.

The rest remained behind an impenetrable wall, like the barrier that had fallen across the continent with the old country locked away on the other side. An experience formed of trauma, fear and confusion remained unrelated: the terror of blitzkrieg and the armoured division's desperate fighting retreat in the shadow of the Tatra. The parents he would never see again – mother weeping, imploring him to leave them behind. The creeping awareness of entrapment as news arrived of the Soviet invasion in the east. The executions of his compatriots by bands of Gestapo and NKVD, hunting them down like prey through mountain passes.

And he never spoke of the battles that followed with a different division, through Normandy, Belgium and the Netherlands, except for the sweetness of witnessing his enemy's surrender at Wilhelmshaven. The fabric of that world was too violently torn, the men who travelled there with him erased, disfigured or also silent.

The city of his birth was now in a country with a different name, its inhabitants dead or removed to the ruins of Breslau. Paweł's world had been here, with his books and his handful of relics, and Mary in her armchair.

~

In 1949, at the age of twenty-two, Mary was living a cyclical life of long, punishing days on her parents' farm in Galway. It fell on her to feed the livestock, tend the vegetable crops, keep house and raise her five younger siblings. Everything, it seemed. Frankly, her mother was worn out.

Poverty barely described their life there. A diet of bread and potatoes, mainly, with most of the meat and the uncracked eggs going to market. Dirty all the time – a bath once a week by the fire on Saturday night, but only to impress at Mass on Sunday morning. The ever-present risk of infections – from too many people in damp, cramped houses and shared beds with sacks for sheets. Or just feeling ill from the filth, rain and fatigue. And what did the future hold for a woman there? Working just to subsist, then perpetual pregnancy. A life controlled by men who always got what they wanted and priests who slurred you as unclean because you submitted.

And Mary knew there was a better life, too. Care packs came from family in Boston, America, with dolls in pretty dresses and shiny cast-metal toy cars. The accompanying letters told stories of a life of plenty – even for people like them.

Then a letter arrived from an uncle in an English city, with a tempting proposition. Things were looking up there too, in spite of the destruction wrought by war. Uncle John was a bricklayer – reconstruction had started, there was plenty of work. Aunt Maggie was a midwife with the new health service. They were training nurses in their thousands, she said, and paying them well. And here was the crux of it. The tenement they'd lived in since the twenties had been demolished. They'd been rehoused in a flat that was 'like a palace.' Pat was doing his national service so it was only the girl at home, one of the rooms was vacant. So that was it, a pitch for rent, but no bother. Seeing nothing for herself in Ireland, Mary accepted the offer and joined the exodus.

In the flat on Edward Street she found herself immersed in an immigrant community with St Vincent's Church at its core. Slum clearances had thinned out the population but the Masses were still crowded. Feast day processions along Solly Street provided entertainment and a balm for homesickness. And while the church brought the community together, it wasn't the fearsome, controlling force she'd experienced in Ireland.

Her life at the Royal Hospital was her own, and no one stopped her going to dances at the City Hall ballroom on Saturday nights. But the skinny lads there, with their clumsy chat and Brylcreemed hair, were just an amusement. Besides, her nursing was everything for the moment. And she knew that even if she did marry, only the wrong man would tell her to pack it in the day after.

~

At the end of hostilities Paweł remained with the occupying forces in northern Germany until 1947. But he knew returning home would be impossible. The Soviet Union had consumed his city. The communists, whom he hated, would shoot him as an enemy of the state or, at best, send him to the Gulag. Katyn was a constant, menacing reminder. But the Resettlement Act was fortuitously timed, granting him citizenship along with thousands of his exiled compatriots. It was his engineering degree from the Politechnika Lwowska and a good word from a former comrade that brought him to the city, to take up a job at the East Hecla works.

On Sunday 29th November 1953 Paweł was still finding his feet – lodging in an austere attic room on Spring Hill, striving to decipher the norms and unspoken rules of a society that continued to bewilder, negotiating prejudice veiled with friendliness. Attending Mass with a work colleague, a twenty-minute walk away on Solly Street, was a hesitant attempt at integration.

St Vincent's, too, was piecing itself back together after the war. The windows, organ and altar had just been restored following their destruction in the bombing raid of 12th December 1940. To honour both its centenary and restoration, more than a thousand people crammed into the church for High Mass, celebrated by the bishop of a neighbouring city.

Paweł had certainly noticed the young woman with blonde curls and a white floral dress on the pew beside him. But in the gloom of survival and exile, his confidence eroded, there was only a momentary thought – that such loveliness was beyond his reach. He noticed her glancing at him, this strange outsider, as his tongue tripped on the words of Be Thou My Vision. But when he looked back she smiled mischievously, radiating warmth. A game ensued of increasingly silly expressions – stuck out tongues and pursed lips – finally dissolving into repressed laughter.

Later, both would look back on that moment as one of divine intervention – the unseen hand of a greater being subtly moving the pieces together, revealing the final destination of two uncertain journeys.

They married quickly. By 1954, the year of their wedding, neither was young by the standards of the time – Paweł thirty-six and Mary twenty-seven. They made a home together – a white-rendered semi with bay windows and a long, tree-lined garden. Paweł insisted on painting the front door and facias in a particular shade of red. In time, three boys would be stacked rowdily in the larger bedroom, the girl on her own in the tidy box room – sparsely furnished with a lamp, a bible and a pile of Enid Blytons.

When a woman loves and nurtures with complete devotion, the boundaries of the self can seem to exist far beyond those of the body. In an age when homemaking could still be enough, Mary's identity as a mother and wife was inseparable from the physical reality of home. In a way felt, but never articulated, the house was in unity with her body, her womb – a place for continual growth and nourishment. And it slowly became clear to her that for Paweł, without his conscious intent, it was becoming a museum of memories, a projector screen for the preservation of images from an old, irredeemably lost world.

Through the house's artefacts and photographs, the memories embedded in its walls and surfaces, its echoes and aromas, through their shared experience of exile and creation, Mary and Paweł melded together – becoming an integrated whole.

And so to be taken from here, to leave the house in the hands of others who would unpick its fabric to build their own world, was to face the deletion of her and Paweł's existence – the only one she knew.

At some point the sale would go through. And yes, she was bitter, selfishly taking no joy in a young couple's prospects of happiness.

The clatter of needles stopped. The unfinished piece lay crumpled in her lap, the knit unravelling.

Life's fixtures fade away like sun-bleached photographs, or transform beyond recognition. Sometimes, suddenly, they disappear. There's an image of the final Mass at St Vincent's, in July 1996. It shows the priest carrying the altar stone before him, walking for the last time towards the church door. That could be Mary there – the woman in early old age who seems to be wiping away a tear. Afterwards the church fell into ruin, before its resurrection as a meeting place for a new generation of immigrants, this time from more distant countries. I like to think some of them, too, have found their cure for loneliness there.

The Quest

Times and practices were changing in this city made from metal. Out by the motorway, on a new technology park, researchers were pioneering new approaches in the age-old quest – for ever-greater integrity and strength.

A team of professors and post-graduates, engineers and materials scientists, they'd moved on now from iron and carbon enhanced with alloying elements – manganese, chromium, vanadium or silicon. These days even the finest steel was just a commodity.

Instead they'd embraced an alien technology, borrowed from the city of cotton and the dobby loom, to form a multi-dimensional weave: the warp and the weft with a binder for added strength, the x, y and z axes.

All set in a hard matrix – for toughness and resistance to impact.

The Originals

If ever there were any Originals here, they were a motley lot from the start, cobbled together from genetic material gathered in Germania, France and Scandinavia, remote regions of the Roman empire, the province of Britannia and the home territory of Brigantia itself.

They occupied a smattering of villages and hamlets, each with a unique specialism – forging or grinding, sickles, scythes, scissors or knives. Over time the settlements expanded and collided, accreting like a celestial body. The largest planetesimal of them all acquired the greatest gravity, attracting and coalescing with the others, melting them together in the heat of its furnaces. Bringing a town into being.

The town's voracious factories gorged on resources, massifying, driving yet more attraction and growth. Capital and labour, producers, traders, administrators and religious saviours, but most of all manual workers, arriving as granular individuals or ready-made congregations.

The early migrants came from satellite villages, the novel names in parish registers revealing their local origins – Bamford, Barnsley, Hoyland, Oxspring. But in a smaller, less connected world these were identifiable outsiders, with alien manners and voices, no doubt unsettling an established population that imagined itself indigenous.

In the nineteenth century the town's population grew sevenfold – global dominance could only be achieved with imported manpower. Revolutions in production scale demanded entire new labour forces to power the immense mills that multiplied along the lower valley. They travelled west from agricultural flatlands, making homes near workplaces or where the train stopped: their displaced, rural minds more readily moulded to the needs of capital than those of the city's hustling, home-working anarchs – clocking in, clocking out, doing as they were told.

More exotic elements were sprinkled into the mix: Frenchmen summoned by an earl for their skills with charcoal furnaces and forges, cutlers, watchmakers and pork butchers from the Rhineland and Austria-Hungary; the Italians and Jews of St Vincent's, mingling with the Irish who arrived here on foot from the port of Liverpool.

These were the city's Outsider and Original tribes of the Industrial Revolution, divided by discrete cultures and experiences, honed in the heavy and light trades and supporting services. In time they'd blend together into a single citizenry – sharing dialect words and native traditions, drinking together on St Mondays, superficially homogeneous. All of them Originals now.

∾

After the last war, the city lay in ruins, exhausted and hollowed out by austerity. But newcomers continued to arrive, like the demobbed Polish soldier whose old home had been annexed by the Soviet Union. Reconstruction led to recovery then manpower shortages – on the transport system, in the factories and the new health service.

Not for the first time – there are earlier, infamous examples – men and women of the colonies were called on for cheap labour. Appeals went out via official channels, formally inviting them to help rebuild their mother country, at the heart of their Empire – the one many of them had just fought for. Thousands arrived in the city from the Caribbean, the Middle East, South East Asia and the Indian subcontinent, carrying passports in which it was written that they too belonged here.

Patterns repeat in their stories like in ancient myths. Men came alone at first, on forays from villages in Jamaica, Yemen or West Pakistan. The city they encountered was incomprehensible – strange customs described in a baffling dialect. Shifts were long and hard, in filthy foundries and machine shops. To the boss you were a cheap factor input, to the union an unwelcome inconvenience. When the women arrived, they found isolation in rented slums with rising damp. In the streets there were stares, insults and often worse.

Sad eyes and hanging heads betrayed the crushing disappointment – that the land of milk and honey promised in those distant classrooms had been cruelly mis-sold. Even so, the natives here would never accept you as equals.

But then this blurred, incoherent world came into focus. You began to learn the ropes. With friends from the old country you built a community centre, studied the language, helped each other out. A trip home might have revealed your memories to be rose-tinted – nothing was like before, only the problems. So you came back and carried on. In the end you settled down, because life can't progress with temporary arrangements. Besides, people want the usual things – a house, a family, stability, prosperity even.

The city's new communities clustered together – close to work, for security and support, to replicate the neighbourhoods and networks they'd left behind.

They still do. On demographic maps, swatches of indigo show the highest concentrations of minorities – around the city centre, stretching out to the northern estates and the East End. They overlap with similar swatches on similar maps, representing deprivation in its multiple forms – low incomes, poor health, lives cut short.

These tapestries of disadvantage remind us that immigrants settle where the lodgings are cheap, places more established citizens choose to leave. To some they reveal a reluctance to integrate. But it's an observation that cuts both ways – the Anglo Saxons have their maps too, with their own zones of deep blue – places where we like to keep ourselves to ourselves.

Besides, indigo swatches can be misleading. In most of these districts the minorities are just that – in the minority. What the maps really describe is a city divided, between relative wealth and equal-opportunities poverty – available to the less privileged irrespective of their origins.

Those migrant dreams of prosperity weren't to last. What came next was gradual but inexorable economic collapse. A shabby seventies disco where the four-on-the-floor slowly fell to pieces, barely stayin' alive, transitioning to a synthetic sound of digital trills and immaterial beats – metal on metal made obsolete. Where the last track was performed by an unmanly man in lipstick and earrings – unwanted, unable to believe he was no longer needed. A switch had been tripped. Groups of recent arrivals stood exposed in the spotlights, in their flared jeans and different skins. Lost in time and space, the last bus home already departed.

Over by the bar, the Originals stared into their pints with expressions of disbelief. It wasn't supposed to happen like this. The Empire had sheltered their forebears behind its barricades, churning out steel for mighty dreadnoughts and captive, colonial railways. Its lingering, lifted wealth had kept things cushy – jobs for life on union terms in zombie industries. These were children of the greatest imperium the world had ever seen – feelings of specialness ran deep. Hadn't their dads won the war, all by themselves, not long since? Weren't they still celebrating, in films with basic, binary moralities?

But now they were queuing in Job Centres, then stacking supermarket shelves, with blokes called Delroy and Abdul who only came here to sweep up the turnings. These were things with the power to irritate.

Deprived of colonies we sought new ways to buck the system – to still have the cake, loaded with jam and cream, that we'd already eaten. In desperation we joined the Continental Club, demanding terms suited to our exceptionalism. But the deal, unthinkably, had two sides. With the city on its uppers, the migrants kept on coming.

This time they came from Czechia, Slovakia, Poland, Latvia and Spain, to serve in hospitals, pharmacies and care homes, to clean windows, build houses and operate machines. The poor Roma followed to fill another vital vacancy – giving the rest of us someone else to blame. And all the while this proud city of sanctuary extended its hand to refugees, from wars in Somalia, the Congo, Iraq and Afghanistan (we didn't even start all of them).

To which the underemployed Original might have responded:

'Okay, but what about me?'

In a chuntering population the post-imperial tantrum was delayed but inevitable. The walls of our fortress had been breached, the invaders were to blame for our misery (or so said a millionaire banker in tailored tweeds). And we knew them so little that most of us could believe it. They stayed on their patches, we stayed on ours, never the twain should meet. The city voted as a microcosm of the country – to set Britannia free, albeit narrowly.

The revolution threw up a curious alliance – between Originals and a segment of Outsiders who saw an opportunity – finally to assert the equal standing that should always have been theirs, that was written in their parents' passports, not to mention their own. Now, a different tribe would be beyond the pale. Now they could join the ranks of the Originals.

But soon the whole performance was exposed as a con trick, and angry Original Ultras were smashing up mosques that had stood for decades (not here though – it's not this city's thing). The lesson: Originals versus Outsiders is a dangerous game, because most of its players will judge you by your looks, even if you were born here.

In the park, representatives of the city's tribes cluster on their picnic rugs, cooking distinctive cuisines on instant barbecues, separated by empty expanses. Incompletely coalesced. Reshuffled and reoriented, this could be a vast map of the city's districts.

My wife crosses an invisible boundary to speak to a friend from the school gate – one of the few places where the city's diverse elements alloy together. But they also share connections to more southerly climes, with similar perspectives on the primacy of family and daily routines still influenced by intolerable midday heat. You could find either of them by duck ponds or in supermarket aisles at half past six, when the Anglos are at home having tea. She relates her father's story of moving here from Pakistan in the late sixties – one of the invitees – and his life of hard work and doing without for his kids.

She's there with her own – students of medicine and engineering – the next generation of net contributors.

On the way to the car we pass an extended family of West Africans. A small boy leaves the group and runs towards me, smiling. His father jumps up and dashes after him, then pulls him away. 'Be careful', he says. There's work still to do here, evidently.

~

The Originals isn't an objective category of people. It's more a way of thinking that any of us with imagined origins here can slip into. It involves proneness to a romantic fantasy – that authentic citizens sit on the branches of an extended family tree, one of native species, with its stock established firmly in native soil. It follows that citizens with obviously different origins are unbelonging, parasitical, in the extreme, hanging on conspicuously like human mistletoe. But the real city of people demands a different analogy – mineral, astronomical, an agglomeration of once disparate elements, almost none of which come from around here, all of which are integral.

A similar, comforting illusion applies to the built city – the one of streets, parks, houses and workplaces – imagined as a robust construction that grows and develops through time like a progressing but eternally unfinished medieval cathedral. In need of reassurance we grasp at supporting evidence – an old drinking fountain stranded between modern student flats and faculty buildings, vintage steel grates in the streets, stamped with the marks of long-lost municipal utilities. But the real, unreal city floats in a mirage of continual destruction and re-creation, a composition of entirely replacement parts, an authentic Ship of Theseus. Unable to face a reality of impermanence and rootlessness, the Original takes refuge in a soothing dream – the cohesiveness of the city and its people as they used to be, in a golden age before the old truths were undermined, before the world revolved too quickly, before the Outsiders came and spoiled things.

But perhaps herein lies hope of uniting the city's disconnected tribes: the common ailment that afflicts all of us, lurking in the amygdala or some still-to-be-discovered nostalgia bone. The longing for a home that no longer exists, that really never existed, at least in the way we imagine it. It may be for a distant village ringed by mountains, plantations or paddy fields, now absorbed into a megacity's neoplastic suburbs. Or for a post-war council estate where everyone looked like us and looked out for one another – until the Corporation flattened it. This, the melancholic yearning for a home we can never go back to, is our shared inheritance, possibly the most profound human emotion, the sorrow that could bind us together. The city, in its eternal impermanence, belongs to all of us.

Spotting Planes

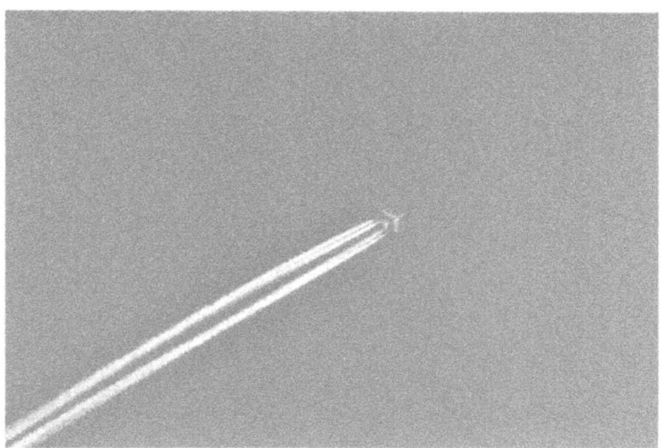

When the Jet Age came the couples traded Filey and Brid for Greece and Spain, flying home with heads full of patios and pretty pots of red geraniums. That was fifty years ago. Ice and rain have punished the patio since then, its once-modish pink, green and yellow slabs cracked and faded beneath years of grime. The rectangle of lawn has lost its perfection – trampled edges, clover, moss and dandelion, a place for playing now.

The brown-eyed boy stands in the sunlight by the lean-to where his father plies his trade. Hammer, anvil, fire and coals. Fibre optics, hard drive, digital runes. The sky above him is infinite blue, the device in his hand a cornucopia of data.

He raises his eyes to the silver silhouettes of jet planes and vapour trails that bloom then dissipate, weaving his world of fascination – carriers and liveries, origins and destinations, exotic global cities with three-letter codes, aircraft types and engine configurations.

'Look: Lublin-Dublin!'

'Manchester-Dubai, A380, you can see, it's got four engines!'

'Frankfurt-New York, Jumbo, that's a cargo flight…'

The warp and the weft. The x, y and z axes.

When the world closed down, they were all cargo flights, and only a few, so he tracked the daily movements of masks, gowns and ventilators from country to country. Solitary, glinting scalpel blades slicing through the blue fabric.

The River – Part Five

The river flows on through its red-brick conduit, behind the pork butcher's, the tyre fitter's and the garage where Ron sat alone in his glass cabin. Inappropriate decor – floral borders. Faded photos – a souped-up Triumph, an eighties beach bar. Self-replicating stacks of service invoices. Ski jacket and frozen feet, running in new knees, sucking in air between his teeth:

'It's a judgement call, like all these things. You could change them now or wait a bit, but I'd say do it before winter.'

Advice as vital as a GP's for a man with a multiply morbid Mercedes.

In the workshop below, Jez – his revs perpetually on the red line – sweats and berates the state of the art.

'Technology,' he says, 'is the rust of the modern age.'

The Soul Messenger

I've no doubt the Matriarch chose the timing of her death. We were all there, gathered around her in the bedroom at the care home. The call had come from the duty manager, but the summons, I think, came from the old lady herself, telepathically, for a final act of communion. For us it was veneration.

She was lying on her side, breathing deeply with the intentionality of a long-distance runner at the limit of endurance. She had waited for us and would continue to hold on. The time had not yet come.

Only her eyes moved, settling on each of us in turn – wide open and penetrating, connecting deep within us, in the infinity beyond the retina. The long seconds when she held me in her gaze immobilised me. A silent interrogation – sceptical, knowing, almost accusing.

Was I, in that moment – in every moment – acting with integrity? she compelled me to ask myself. Were my posture, the tiny movements of my body, my sentiments and the liquid that coated my eyes honest or concocted? Was I there with her completely or were we separated by a barrier of my self-conscious performance? Were my actions truthful or the things I thought I should be doing? Could this peddler of frivolous patter rise to this moment?

Who can guess at the contents of that vestibule between the physical and immortal worlds? Did they blend together, with her grandmothers Kitty and Clara, her first love and the Sailor, her parents and brothers all standing there among us? Or, in the moments when her eyes were closed, did they beckon her, waiting beyond an immaterial threshold, or silhouetted behind a curtain of intangible fabric?

And was that waiting room the auditorium of an ethereal picture palace – the Adelphi or the Electra, perhaps – with a clattering projector and a screen of light showing silent, moving images of waypoints along the road – the music shop and the bustling Common, the Circle and the pale-yellow kitchen, the Sundial Club and rose beds in the garden at Hallowmoor? A silent film punctuated with cliffhangers, telling the story of a life lived well and a city's troubled century – of decline and fall and endurance.

When the time came, in a way that can't be enunciated, everything was correctly positioned. It was as though the piece – the rite of passage – had been orchestrated through an intense exercise of will. The meticulously assembled finale to an elegant composition. The exact moment of crossing was unknowable. It had already passed when I heard my aunty's hushed but anxious words:

'Mum? No, don't go Mum.'

A shadow at the edge of my visual field drew my eyes away from her. I have perfect recall of a majestic bird with wings extended swooping towards the window, then ascending almost vertically to disappear over the rooftop. The mythical soul messenger had made her collection.

I wonder if, in her final moments, she was comforted by the familiarity of the setting – close to their first home on Mason Lathe Road, the point of departure for a different, momentous journey seventy-six years before.

The walls and windows of this building were new but the view over the woods and the garden estate was older. It belonged to the lounge of the hotel where she and her first husband had sat with friends at their favourite corner table. Her with a bottle of Guinness and a lady's glass, my grandfather with a pint of ale.

∾

The composition, we were soon to discover, ended with an unexpected coda.

The old lady's family members hadn't been the only companions with her that afternoon. Propped up on the dressing table, next to the television, were two additional participants: a koala and a rhino.

There's some truth in the notion that extreme old age is a return to childhood, so it's easy to dismiss her fondness for this stuffed, furry duo as infantile. But these were relationships maintained with a gentle, self-aware sense of humour. Anyway, she was alone in a small room with prescience of the falling darkness. Looking to them for comfort, like a young girl in a dark, music shop attic, wasn't such a strange thing to do.

I'd noticed that as her eyes moved from one of us to the next they had settled on the gap between me and my brother. But there was no one there, at least according to the conventional, unmagical definition of a person.

Three days after her mortal remains were removed from the room, in that liminal phase between death and funeral, the care home receptionist received a call – an interrogation by an assertive female.

Where were Kate's stuffed toys? she demanded. The rhino and the koala? They were missing. The receptionist said she had no idea but would look into it. The call ended abruptly: the click of an old-fashioned receiver, a continuous tone.

When my mother called at the home to say thank you to the carers, the duty manager couldn't apologise enough. They'd looked all over, she said. They had no idea where they were. Mum looked at her nonplussed. She hadn't made the call, neither had her sister, and no one else knew about the toys or their apparent importance.

There could only be one conclusion: the soul messenger had messed up; negligently, the companions the Matriarch wished to accompany her on her journey to the next world had been left behind. And she was disgruntled, like an Egyptian queen opening her immortal eyes to see an empty tomb. The battleaxe was battling on. More likely, though, the caller had been hard to identify because it's hard to speak when your tongue's in your cheek. She was teasing us, reminding us gently that while the room and the bed were empty, she remained with us.

Now, the rhino sits in our spare bedroom, on top of the wardrobe, observing us from either side of a fluffy white horn while we're ironing shirts or scribbling tales. And she'll probably sit there forever. Because we know who's keeping a loving eye on us. And because, truth be told, none of us would dare move her.

The Barbed Wire Picket

Superficially, Redmires is just another ravaged upland landscape: deforested by ancient men or a cooling climate, engineered for industrial-scale water management, planted with rows of soulless conifers, scarred by the tools of road builders, quarrymen and doomed citizen soldiers. At its fringes the heather moorland is slashed, burned and spoiled for the entertainment of a tacky visiting elite – new money dressed up as old.

But it pays to look more closely. Because this is a place where messages from the dead are etched into mileposts, paving stones and the earth itself, where, in the wake of all these human interventions, ley lines of memory and meaning intersect and overlap.

I'm here on a cool, sunlit day in April, climbing the grassy slope to Quarry Hill. On the north side I find traces – shallow indentations in the ground, all that remains of the battalion's complex network of training trenches. A skylark hovers over me, then plunges, swoops and rises again, transmitting his secret signal through the ages – a continual stream of arcane trills and bleeps, the data of a timeless witness unburdened.

Back on the road I follow the edge of the upper dam. A watcher sits in silence on his usual bench: flat cap, anorak, gaze fixed on the water – mercury with flakes of gold. Another day in a rich man's retirement of solitary walks and contemplation, packed up with ham sandwiches wrapped in tin foil.

From the reservoir's south-west corner I head uphill on the stony track of the Long Causeway – a Roman road or a medieval trading route for packhorses carrying cutlery, galena or Cheshire salt – whichever story we choose to tell.

After a mile or so, at the top of the moor, a tall wooden pole – here in some form for almost five hundred years – marks the boundary between two counties and two ancient kingdoms. To the south, discolourations in the landscape mark the site of the old Flying Corps aerodrome – shadows of its landing strip, living quarters, aircraft repair and transport depots. It was the mission of the pilots based here to defend the city against air attack. But, for whatever reason, they never took off on 25th September 1916, when a Zeppelin laden with bombs passed over this very spot.

Heading back in the direction of the city, the road diverts around the three reservoirs. From this point the old causeway and its milestones were submerged and broken when the dams were built. I continue past the water works, the nature reserve and the farm, then take the footpath along the south side of Redmires Wood, beside the Conduit that once carried water down to the city.

A dog walker emerges from the trees onto the field, following worn trails with the careless confidence that comes with familiarity. I ask if he knows where I'll find the old Redmires Camp. Of course he does.

'Keep going then take the path on the left into the wood. You'll find some interesting things in there'.

Towards the end of the Great War, after the camp had fulfilled its function – preparing the battalion for annihilation – the site was converted to hold prisoners of war. Among them was Karl Dönitz, a sailor of the Imperial German Navy who would later become the second, lesser known and final leader of the Third Reich.

The story begins with a mishap in the Mediterranean in October 1918, when the u-boat under Dönitz's command was forced to surface by the Royal Navy. After a spell in a Maltese prison he was transferred to Redmires, where he passed his time refining the *Rudeltaktik* – for the destruction of convoys by submarines operating in 'wolf packs.'

The image that forms in my mind is, I admit, unrealistic: our proto-Nazi seated at a rustic table in cosy, log cabin accommodation, strategising with pencil and paper in the orange glow of a gas light, attired in the requisite roll-neck sweater and crushed white cap of the cinematic u-boat captain.

An important point to note here is that by this time – the winter of 1918-19 – the war was over. The November Criminals had committed their crimes, the German Empire was defeated. But, with the characteristic grit of a Prussian officer, Dönitz clearly didn't give a damn. Here he was, in the weeks following the armistice, in a prison hut in Redmires (which in reality would have been cold, crowded and miserable), working up his plans for a rematch.

In the 1930s, in response to a localised smallpox outbreak, the camp served as an auxiliary hospital. But it was to be a brief interlude. Before long, and in accordance with Dönitz's apparent wishes, global conflict would recommence, and Redmires Camp would once again be packed with prisoners.

By the end of the war the facility had found its niche – housing POWs with virulent Nazi beliefs. Some were set on escaping, and their tunnel was almost finished. In an overcrowded camp with seventy men sharing huts built for thirty, suspicion multiplied like bacteria. The followers of a creed built on victimisation, once again in thrall to a myth of betrayal, were on the lookout for traitors.

It was in this poisoned environment, in the spring of 1945, that a notorious non-Nazi called Gerhardt Rettig was seen talking to a camp guard through the barbed-wire fence, not far from the undiscovered tunnel's entrance. Threats were overheard, so the camp commander decided to move him for his own safety.

On 24th March, carrying his few possessions in a kit bag, Rettig left his hut for the last time. But immediately he was jumped by a gang of prisoners who beat him until his face was swollen and bleeding. A mob pursued him across the camp and cornered him by the wash house, shouting: 'Traitor!' 'Hang him!' 'Beat him to death!'

As he cowered on the ground, shielding his head with his arms, a boot was repeatedly slammed into his face – splitting his upper lip, exposing the teeth and gums beneath. His assailants doused him with water, dispersing the blood streaming from his mouth and nose, but only to prepare him for the next onslaught. Somehow, he managed to rise to his feet and flee along a passageway between the mess huts and the kitchen.

This, 'the place where rubbish was shot,' according to the prosecuting army officer, was where Rettig was last seen standing, surrounded by a bloodthirsty mob now numbering 'three or four hundred.' He died in an ambulance on the way to one of the city's hospitals. Various causes of death were recorded: severe injuries to the head, asphyxia from the inhalation of blood, 'tearing of the covering of the brain resulting in coma.'

Four inmates were charged with his murder. Two were acquitted and two found guilty, then hanged at Pentonville Prison. One of the convicted men's fanaticism was attributed to a childhood misspent in the Hitler Youth, imbibing Nazi ideology, 'with particular emphasis on the life of the Führer.'

~

There's little to see at first as I turn off the path into the wood – only densely packed Scots pines rising out of an expanse of knotted brambles. Then, as though overcoming vertigo or focusing a camera lens, patches of texture and colour crystallise into meaningful gestalts: sections of concrete lintels protruding from the ground, the coiled tip of a buried barbed wire picket – the type seen in countless images of the Western Front. Then more substantial evidence – a subterranean, brick-lined construction, covered for safety with a plastic road plate: drainage, possibly, or a latrine? Surely too well-engineered for an escapees' tunnel?

Venturing off the path towards the wood's interior I find what I'm searching for: sixty-foot concrete barrack bases arranged in rows, their entrances identified by red-brick steps, obscured by a thin layer of dry leaves, moss and fallen branches. Each one a stage for the lives of cold, hungry, brutalised men – their dreams broken, with nothing to return home to.

Further into the undergrowth, beyond the hut bases, I find the remains of a smaller building – a wash house, perhaps, or a place where rubbish was shot. The sounds of spring surround and absorb me: a bumble bee lazily humming around my midriff, the hopeful bird song of an unseen chorus, a light breeze in the branches – stories overheard from a distance. But still, with the light failing, the atmosphere is heavy and lugubrious. Just to be here, with senses alert, is to know this place has seen wickedness. Because somewhere between these broken walls a man was slaughtered by other men hunting as a mindless pack – humanity in its basest form.

As I stand here among the ruins of prison buildings and the lost hopes of a citizens' army, at the centre of this crime scene, connections and associations accumulate, multiply and almost overwhelm: the barbed wire picket and the battalion's photographed ghosts, the scars of their trenches and the skylark's melancholy notes, the marks of travellers and surveyors on causeway stones, where packhorses crossed paths with lead ore, knife blades and salt. The Flying Corps airstrip and the airship they failed to shoot down, Dönitz with his notebooks and wolf packs, penetrating the armour of convoy ships – rolled at the Atlas Works. The corpses of soldiers and sailors, of the traitor by the rubbish pile, of women, men and children beneath the Zeppelin's blue light and the ridge of the Brigantes.

The Ankh and the Asp

Like many of the city's treasures the library and art gallery is endearingly imperfect: an impure amalgam of styles, falling shy of a Grade 1 listing, isolated, because the wider grand scheme never came off. Now she's neglected, her Portland stone flaking and vintage fittings failing – more a place of sanctuary than culture in these impoverished times.

And yet, in her day, she was a model public building, commissioned by a city still in its pomp (in its imagination, at least), with three libraries and a basement theatre – all state of the art. The top floor gallery exhibited artworks from an expansive city collection, established with a gift of four hundred paintings from a mail order mogul of unusual generosity.

She was built in an age of depression by men of the city who needed work. I like to think the Irish brickies of St Vincent's and Shiregreen were among them – men who, on Corporation house-building sites, taught my great grandfather the drinking songs he performed late at night in a slurred, appropriated brogue.

The place has a feeling of home, and I owe her a debt. As a teenager I studied for exams here, on forays out from our island on the 286, savouring her quiet wisdom – a repository of the city's deeper culture. Later I came here to sketch plans for a small business – extracting myself from a post-redundancy domestic pressure cooker, removing daytime opportunities for my death by mariticide (any reasonable court would have sympathised).

These days I come here on Fridays to scratch out stories: ascending steps with yellow safety nosings, passing through the building's massive threshold – an ancient tomb entrance inverted, arriving in the imposing entrance hall, its shadows and grey pilasters invoking the Temple of Hathor, stepping over the crack that opened in the marble floor at the moment a bomb laid waste to the Marples Hotel.

I glance over at the old lad in the beanie hat playing a wistful *Bring Me Sunshine* on an open-source piano, then swing open a heavy oak door with a tarnished, fantailed brass handle. I surveil the Lending Library then the Reading and Local Studies rooms, searching high and low for a quiet spot, relocating repeatedly to evade sneezers, coughers, throat hockers, farters and compulsive shouters, sometimes even snorers. Finally, I find my place within a gaggle of retired husbands who, once fed, take refuge from their wives in pages of the angling press, at tables that fill up in winter when home heating bills inspire dread. Only then can I pull up my chair to a well-aged oak desk, running eyes and fingers over scratches and blemishes in its seasoned surfaces, imbibing the building and its contents as stores of memory, meaning and lived experience, absorbing the city's essence through the pores of my skin.

So it's perhaps unsurprising that I, like many others in the city, was a little upset when the building's custodians decided to give it away to the first chancer who came along.

∾

The story begins positively enough: a 'signing ceremony' in a faraway country, celebrating a partnership between the city and its big, new overseas investor. An expansive red carpet, guarded by a company of totalitarian pot plants, oversized flags of the Union and the People's Republic, demure hostesses with high buns and red, socialist-sequined evening dresses. And at the centre a familiar Last Supper scene: an extended table covered with a pleated cloth (also in red) and thirteen figures – more or less – seated at, or standing behind it. Everyone's attention is fixed on our very own Great Leader – positioned at the centre, garlanded with flowers, signing… something. I have no idea what, and I suspect she hasn't either. It must be good though, because the businessmen in black suits at her flanks are leaning in and grinning with encouragement:

"Go on. Do it! Do it!"

In her defence this was an investment opportunity too good to miss – a full billion over sixty years, no less. Now, it wasn't entirely clear whether that was a billion in today's money or the diminished currency of six decades hence. A billion's a billion after all, especially when your last accountant was culled in the cuts.

The investment programme would begin with another transformation of the city centre – building fine things like homes, hotels and leisure facilities. As always, hundreds if not thousands of jobs would be created.

A few weeks later it became clear what this transformative cash injection would actually involve. Instead of new projects on any of the city centre's derelict plots the company would, in effect, be given our library and art gallery – to turn into a five-star hotel. Embracing the municipal malnutrition they claimed to despise, our representatives genuflected before the goddess Tina – there is, they insisted, no alternative. While comparable cities had revived the jewels in their public realms, ours was falling down. The repairs would cost millions. So what can you do? Give it away to the first chancer who comes along.

And they were single-minded in their commitment to doing just that. Untruths were told about the existence of a legal agreement, granting the investors time to hatch their plans while thwarting citizens' attempts to secure 'community control' of the building. Corporation representatives, salaried and elected, dissembled and mangled syntax, perpetuating their tawdry myth.

Self-righteous words were mobilised to obscure the great giveaway. The building wasn't 'inclusive' or 'accessible' enough, they said. (Naturally – it hadn't been modernised for eighty years). A new library would be purpose-built – no doubt to the same miserable standards as the new offices in which they'd recently incarcerated their own staff. Nine thousand people weren't buying it and signed a petition to say so.

A splash in the local press revealed the developer's vision: a penile glass tower (the prosthetic of choice for colossal civic inadequates) smashing through the building's central light well (which, for now, illuminates the goings on within), inevitably pulverising the Art Deco interior (although this wasn't mentioned – vulgar facadism in more than one sense). The building would be shafted, literally… its users only metaphorically.

But then, slowly, and in retrospect, inevitably, the facade of the sixty-year investment partnership began to crack.

The investor, it transpired, wasn't the stock market behemoth implied by the Corporation. It was a six-month-old start-up with a name similar enough to confuse, and a director in common.

Unsurprisingly, the company's provenance hadn't been checked out. The Corporation suggested a government agency had done the due diligence, the agency itself wasn't so sure. A picture emerged of a bankrupt country with a titanic hole in its current account, desperate for cash from strangers, kind or otherwise, flashing the bruised thighs of its provincial investment opportunities on the seedy street corners of global financial markets, sucking funny money into its casino to fund dubious developments – from suicidal student flats to wacky library-to-luxury-hotel conversions.

On top of all that, the investors, whoever they were, couldn't get the cash out of their home country. The government there was clamping down on capital flight – to prevent 'money laundering' and 'fake outbound investment transactions.'

A diligent expat journalist dug deeper. The big company investor-that-wasn't was linked to a major scandal at home involving political corruption, financial fraud and – to clinch the malfeasance triple crown – sex. The actual, small-fry investor was only interested in the city because his daughter and son-in-law had studied here. But no one could question their credentials. This entrepreneurial family unit had previously established a 'karaoke experience' in the city – a short-lived enterprise whose assets had been seized by the government.

A Freedom of Information request exposed the Corporation's recklessness in pursuing the deal. They were, it was said, 'desperate to attract investment' and 'blind to the risks.' Still, they dismissed the episode with impressive sang-froid. The project, they said drily, had 'proven more complex and time-consuming than originally anticipated.'

The library and art gallery building provides an astute commentary on her own recent history. Painted on the walls of the central stairwell you'll find quotations expounding the virtues of libraries, inevitably put there by the Corporation itself.

"Libraries gave us power." (The past tense has been noted).

"A library is an arsenal of liberty." (Except when it's an exclusive hotel).

"There is no institution I value more in this country than libraries." (This from a comedian and national treasure who took to the press to describe the Corporation's plans for the building as "a sad reflection on how little the city cares for its public service legacy." They could have painted that on the wall too, but apparently decided not to).

On the building's exterior, high up on a splayed corner, a figure of Knowledge holds in its hands the ankh and the asp, symbolising the choice between good and evil. Straining my eyes I search for evidence of a third, meaning-laden object, perhaps clutched between the figure's exposed knees – something to represent the shabby, compromised middle ground.

∾

At the time of writing the building's facade continues to flake away. Now they've fenced it off. The Portland stone is unsafe, they say, a long-term solution is needed. Some kind of 'review' seems to be in the offing. So, they're regrouping. Softening us up. Preparing for a new offensive.

Here we go. Ready for the next round…

The Guild

In the gilded guildhall a favoured minister had received his applause. Portraits of past Masters lined the walls, displayed between marble pilasters with Corinthian capitals. At a banquet table set with fine cutlery and candelabras a senior member was holding forth, captivating a huddled audience dressed in tailcoats, white ties and winged collars.

I was an interloper – a penguin out of water in a rented suit. So I only caught fragments of their private conversation, hushed words spoken between initiates.

'They think they own this city,' he said, referring to some recent demonstration of the Corporation's authoritarian tendencies.

'But they're wrong. It's ours.' (His admirers guffawed.)

A certain sense of historical privilege reinforced the illusion. But in fact he spoke only of his imagined city, with its own peculiar hierarchy, shared, to a degree, with the men gathered around him – guided by similar maps, identically uniformed. Forgivably, like everyone else, he believed his was the real city. Not just one, without special status, among half a million others.

Fantasy Island

The Island isn't natural, nor is it really an island. It's more of a peninsula, formed by men centuries ago when a goit was cut to drive gristmills, diverting water away from the river. Today, its expanded territory is bounded by the railway line to the north and the ring road to the south – a ribbon of tarmac and traffic only recently sliced through the area, perhaps to the regret of planners now fixated on clean air and active travel.

We used to visit the museum here when we were kids, island hopping on rainy weekends or school trips in pensionable coaches, to marvel at the Bessemer converter – a brutal, mechanical invader from Mars, the aged cutler – performing his trade in a counterfeit workshop, the Grand Slam bomb – made at the River Don Works to exact revenge for obliterated chip shops. The highlight was the massive engine, built to drive armour plate production in the same factory, its nimble switch in direction demonstrated by a gnarled but gentle enthusiast in a greasy cap.

On this occasion we approach the Island on foot from the south, the city centre and the courts complex behind us, the roar and clatter of regeneration punishing our eardrums. Our landing is at the end of Cotton Mill Row, where an all-new Cotton Mill has received its first occupants – lured by a promise of 'urban living at its best', with 'on-trend kitchens' and 'open-plan interiors' that 'balance urban aesthetic and elegance'.

This is progress, no doubt. The Cotton Mill's original iteration – an 'unsightly edifice' – was repurposed in 1829 as the city's Union Workhouse. At the time of the flood, in 1864, it held more than a thousand inmates, mostly – following Victorian convention – women or the insane (or both), incarcerated behind giant gates secured with iron bars. The flood inundated grim ground-floor rooms including the children's, smallpox and venereal wards, and a store stuffed with corpse-filled coffins awaiting burial. It's said that the lunatics quartered on the same level, for once with sound reason, wailed as the water began to rise.

On Russell Street we encounter our first islander – a woman walking a toy dog in a pink coat. (To be clear, the dog's wearing the pink coat). The woman looks a little uncomfortable, scuttling back from the bins down a designer backstreet called Makers Place, marooned in a showpiece of fashionable living between a mattress outlet, a self-storage shed and a car park secured by industrial fencing.

I'm sceptical about these newly built eco-houses. For my own home I selected a bomb-proof, thirties semi, constructed from undrillable refractory bricks. I suspect only the purchasers here, at a push, are fully invested in the sustainability mission, that the builder's enthusiasm for plywood, plastic membrane and corrugated sheeting is differently motivated.

Our route takes us through a neighbourhood in the throes of radical change, where buildings are transforming, ascending or expiring, new activities and cohorts replacing or rubbing along with the old, bursts of colour lighting up the faded greys, browns and dark reds of residual industry.

Prime riverside sites now accommodate modern apartment blocks with gated car parks. An old brick and stone cutlery works and a saw and file factory are adapted to office and residential uses. Death Row industrial units with asbestos roofs declare clamping in operation – awaiting the bulldozer. Curated murals and graffiti adorn the walls of a reworked steelworks – stylised sunbursts between smokestacks, an impressionist forest, a burns victim bursting through a brick wall, the effect sullied, or enhanced, perhaps, by dissident scribbles on a louvred, plant room door.

A Spring Factory that used to be a spring factory now houses a community of makers and doers. A sign outside gives warning of a PR company in residence. Among the dereliction, hip new businesses are springing up – street food halls and flea markets, artisan bakeries and microbreweries, vintage clothing and antiques emporia.

Cafes, bars and kitchens display names evocative of thankless toil that kills you before you're thirty – grind and graft in badly ventilated workshops. Here, wearing a stylish reproduction of proletarian headgear, you can idle and sip an elderflower cocktail, oblivious to the proximity of sweaty metals-trade holdouts – hard-faced hardfacers, surface coaters, shot blasters, welders and fabricators.

From appearances it's easy to construct a fantasy of textbook gentrification – of trailblazing bohemian artists with guerilla studios in abandoned machine shops, of investors and developers following in their wake, cashing in on the cool they'd warmed up, then a later wave of affluent arrivals, embedding the district's bougie credentials.

But it didn't really happen like that. Because the Island we see today was the product of a top-down vision, a planned and coordinated project from the start. The coalition of midwives attendant at its birth included one-time socialist Corporation councillors and their planning officers – redirecting evangelism from social housing to aspirational loft living, the city burghers who crammed the boards of regeneration agencies – feeding from multiple troughs, an endlessly regenerating elite of grey suits, affected lisps and chiffon scarves, and groundbreaking developers with keen noses for grant-assisted growth opportunities.

Inspiration came from places like Brooklyn – a down at heel workers' neighbourhood colonised and made respectable by the professional classes – which, incidentally, lent its name to an early scheme here, based on a tenuous historical association.

Visitors to the Island today might imagine a homogeneous community of hipsters. But nowhere's as simple as it seems on the surface, and this place is home to multiple, overlapping tribes.

The real pioneers weren't so much radical creatives as members of an estate agent's segment called *young professionals* – in the early, peripatetic stages of careers, drawn to an affordable first wave of housing and a context more rousing than their suburban origins. No doubt they were accompanied by a smattering of divorcees, squeezing the max from half of what they used to have, resuscitating less mundane pre-marital lives.

The older crowd we see today, with their sculpted beards, calfskin-patched donkey jackets and cashmere wives, came more recently – drawn by a later round of higher-end developments, the potential for price inflation proven, the prostitutes pushed out to the fringes. These are the gentrifiers from central casting – financially sorted managers from the creative, media or digital sectors, embracing labelled iterations of urban fashions that were edgy two decades since.

But even 'hipster' isn't a cohesive category. Because the affluent fraction with their plug-in vehicles and double ovens is waited on – in stylish delis, hair salons and vegan restaurants – by an associated but materially different sub-tribe – their tattoos less inhibited, creeping onto to their faces, their ears misshapen by large-gauge piercings too risqué for client meetings.

This is a new, esteemed service and small business class, with taste and talent (like the southern Italians of old) but without a pot to piss in. Rooted in the skilled working classes or the downwardly mobile middle, they're disenfranchised by the financial crash and alienated from the suburbs by exploding house prices. Shut out from conventional dreams or maybe just bored by them, they're drawn to creative, manual endeavours as makers of bespoke jewellery or exquisite pastries, turning their backs on fifty-grand degrees that line you up only for life in a cheap suit, surveilled, desperate for a pee, in an outbound call mill. And as in every quarter where the young and fiscally-stretched search for their places, they're hunted by missionaries from a megachurch that makes worship fun. Because God only knows why they've failed to replicate the standards of living their parents gave them.

Were this a typical case of gentrification, there would also be a resident underclass, clinging on by their unscrubbed fingernails, slowly but inexorably getting forced out. But there isn't, much, for the simple reason that hardly anyone lived on the Island before its reinvention. (Those who once did were driven out decades ago, by the expansion of industry or state-directed slum clearances).

Instead, the candidates for displacement are 'low-value' metal-bashing firms, their insalubrious accommodation a source of irritation to planners set on realising their architectural pornographics. The tribe that comes with them – yet to be exterminated – is a daytime population of ageing males: dressed in swarf-ingrained blue overalls that may or may not be authentic, eating snap from white-bread bags, dropping in to unrefurbished pubs for pints after work.

Some of those establishments are run by members of the original real ale tribe, whose independent breweries preceded the first residential conversions. Perhaps they were the middle-class advance guard, with their no-smoking rooms and fruit machine bans (although the trend for industrial re-enactment started at the museum).

But these hairy beer-men in cords and Aran sweaters were hardly cool, and their pubs are among the few places where the island tribes seem to mix with a degree of comfort. There you can still find a cheap pint and a decent, no-frills meal, and you'll still see old lads in the tap room with indigenous accents and clothes that are just old, escaping while their wives cook the Sunday roast. Outside in the more modish beer garden you might spot a pair of metropolitan refugees, wearing designer shades and the expressions of the not-entirely-convinced.

If anything the real ale crowd are the linchpins of this community: merging with both the professionals and the antediluvian manual workers, engaging in relaxed interactions with the younger, trendier craft beer crew – united by a love for complex hop aromas, softening their opinions on kegs and CO2.

Above all, because both the city's old guard and the newcomers are essentially liberal, tolerance seems to be pervasive. I read a report somewhere of apartment residents' cars being vandalised and sprayed with the words 'poshies out.' Which begs the question: which of the Island's tribes could possibly have been responsible? It certainly wasn't Dave from the (industrial) welding shop – the language alone is ridiculous, a shrug would be a more likely response, or at worst a light-hearted quip about posers. Instead my imagined culprits belong to an underground cell of trust fund Trots: late arrivals posturing as the urban vanguard, enduring heavy, post-university hangovers, ensconced in bogus, designer squats, fighting fake battles for illusory victims from a seventies sociology textbook.

But I need to stop here and take a step back, because something's bothering me. It's the metropolitans in the beer garden, frozen, in spite of expensive, matching ski jackets, looking for all the world like they're thinking: 'My God, darling, what have we done?'

Did they come here having read a review in the national press, positioning this neighbourhood at the pinnacle of an urban cool ranking (written, perhaps, by a young debutante from the soft-furnished comfort of a West End flat following a fleeting, virtual visit)? Had they not understood that the Island will be delightful when it's finished, in the city that never will be finished?

Here's something else I read about this place: some of the people who come to live here say they're attracted by its 'authenticity.' But the problem with authentic authenticity, at least in a city like this, is that it can be miserable, and raise serious health and safety concerns. So the Cotton Mill, with its passably quaint associations, is referenced selectively, but no one wants to live on Madhouse Mews or sip espressos in the Venereal Ward Cafe. The reimagined Island obliterates, rather than invokes, the past. It's a stage set built by prissy social engineers, inhabited by obliging troupes of players costumed as parodic proles, with all the verisimilitude of musical theatre. It's a venue for performance, where incredible origin myths are acted out before our eyes. Another island of artifice, prefabricated from fantasy.

I like the Island, nevertheless. Its bridges, weirs, mill race and yards with scrap metal bins stimulate an ancient part of the brain. I'm emotionally attached to cask conditioning and surface engineering, and thank its vendors for raising the street food bar (critics of hipster hospitality should remember its antecedents). The engine, switching direction, touches my soul. I love a unique hand tool collection as much as the next middle-aged man.

There's just one thing that grates a bit. This is a cool city, but the 'cool' recently introduced to the Island (and closely associated with the industries of deception) sits uncomfortably within it. The adjective stands, the noun's an imposter. The problem with cool is taking itself too seriously – which explains why it feels alien here. But this city has an incorrigible habit of reasserting itself – disarming self-regard with gentle humour, fettling the edges off pretension. As the Island becomes a magnet for diners, drinkers and perusers, the city bleeds back into it, reseeding the ground with vernacular culture. Before we know it the posers will be taking the piss out of their own daft haircuts.

And as with any other system-built suburb, moss will grow between the new, immaculate bricks, architects' plans will be subjected to genius adaptations by eccentric, untameable individuals. Authenticity, finally, will be born of contrivance. And something real will emerge in spite, not because of, the planners' confections.

The River – Part Six

The river flows between the nursing home (we saw a rat by the bins there) and the General Cemetery, where the city's great men rest uneasily in broken tombs. A Doric gateway spans a Styx of chip trays and fly-tipped pallets. A homeless bloke rocks on a discharge pipe, his tent pitched behind him in the bushes. Tiers of curved catacombs sit vacant – Victorian demand misread, harder to shift than they thought. All around, headstones are laid down, toppled by high-vis contractors for the prevention of further deaths.

Up on the hill a blackened stone chapel melds Greek and Egyptian. Behdety, the winged sun god, shines down, surveying his city of alchemy.

St Valentine's Day

At the city's western fringe, on a hilltop facing the prevailing winds, a great cavity slices into the earth. These days it's a peaceful place, traversed by walkers and cyclists on asphalt paths, its brutal history and outcrops of rock softened by civilising rows of park benches.

This was the bole – a massive hearth hewn out of the ground for the smelting of lead, the woods all around coppiced for fuel, powerful westerlies harnessed for blast to raise the heat of hell.

Galena was carried here by packhorse. Toiling men laid down blocks, then blackwork, shankards and brash burdened with fresh ore. The fire burned for days, the molten metal flowing away and cooling into solid ingots. Each firing – conducted by breathless, blackened smelters with short lives ahead of them – consumed tens of tons of fuel and feedstock.

But what am I doing here on this cold, clear February afternoon? Only watching, like everyone else. Sitting silently in this amphitheatre of dark, quarried rock and backfilled earth, captivated by a performance for which no fees were levied, no incentives distributed. A city resting after years of hard labour.

Twin rivers twist away along their deep, glowing valleys, touching black patches of dams at the horizon. Fragments of sunlight glint on a trilogy of tower blocks rising up from a spillover hillside. At Long Lane, a sixties vision of future living squares up to an archaic world of dry stone walls, populated by lonely ponies and vacationing urban cats.

But most eyes look up to the dilute sky where vapour trails stream like liquid lead. Huddled couples shiver here instead of at home – you might as well watch planes when you can't pay the heating bill. Words overheard – gently idle observations, spoken as though time sets no limits.

'Look, they're crossing over each other.'

'Those two are making an equals sign…'

St Valentine's day, and nowhere could be more romantic.

Glimpsing a square of worn-out lawn through a tangle of bushes I feel sure the Matriarch roamed here – that bus-pass Bedouin of all the city's parks and bowling greens, rapporteur of foot-fault scandals at Mulehouse Road, Firth Park, High Hazels and similar exotic oases. I could see her sitting here with the Sailor, side by side on a green bench at the Scenic Point, her in a beige Rackham's Mac, him in a blue-grey anorak. Watching carefully, contemplating quietly. Important things they still knew how to do in those days.

The Sailor's Valley

A golden morning in May and our latest quest: to find the site of the old dam that failed with catastrophic consequences. I'm keen but my young co-traveller seems less invested. On these walks I suspect he slips unconsciously into the role of carer, wearing that expression sometimes seen in waiting rooms and shopping centres: 'don't worry about him, he's safe.'

We leave the old Merc by the lane and follow the path down through the woods to the embankment, built in the 1870s after its predecessor's collapse. But the route across the dam wall is sealed off – locked gates, spikes, warning signs: 'in the interest of public safety… strictly no access…'

A friendly family – mum, dad, lad, Pomeranian lapdog ('watch her, she'll have your leg off') – tells us that the water company only recently barred access. It might have been out of altruistic concern for hikers and wild swimmers, or possibly following an exercise to quantify the level of risk they'd tolerate. Zero. But I suspect the global bankers and investment fund managers who now control what once belonged to the City Corporation – and therefore, more or less, to us – have little interest in the welfare of rambling lecturers and skinny-dipping students. The real message is simpler: this is ours, not yours, so piss off. The freeholder's compulsion to enclose.

It's apparent that mother's the fearless NCO in this plucky platoon.

Sturdy and purposeful in black and pink lycra. Cool in gold-mirrored sports sunglasses. Not one to mess with. If they ever come here, which they won't, the company executives might be disconcerted by the natives' contempt for their corrals and notices.

She explains how her squad rises to the landowner's challenge. Climb over the barbed wire fence and walk along the sloping dam wall by the waterline. The Canada Geese get a bit snappy – best keep your fingers in your pockets. The signs and metal spikes are all on the path over the dam top, so presumably no one minds. Chuckle. On the other side you have to cross the spillway and climb a metal ladder – it's about twelve feet high but easy enough.

I'm in awe. The kid's about eight and dad, wearing flip flops, is no bantamweight. And what about the Pomeranian? Does it hang around someone's neck for these commando escapades? Whatever the tactics, good-humoured radical trespassing is at the heart of their Sunday walks. On her phone Mum shows us photos of the derelict industrial buildings they've broken into together. As a family. Better than day trips to Legoland, I reckon.

The replacement embankment was built about three hundred yards up the valley from the original. In between the land shows the usual signs of disturbance by man in the distant past, like a bole or an Iron Age hill fort. Soil eroded, trees stunted, rock faces excavated. A dispiriting facsimile of a natural river course – pallid water seeping over concrete weirs, bounded by surly, stone retaining walls. Botched surgical reconstruction.

Walking back up the hill towards the road we spot the sign we'd missed, carelessly, on the way down – an arched marker stone engraved with four letters: CLOB.

∾

The initials stood for Centre Line Old Bank, marking where the old dam wall briefly spanned the valley. Below us, a hundred and sixty years before, in a spot now obscured by vegetation, the Waterworks Company's senior engineer had inspected a crack in the new embankment.

Wind and rain had whipped the reservoir all day. Outlet pipes had been opened to release thousands of gallons of water. But still waves crashed over the dam top. The by-wash – a side channel designed to prevent overflow – wasn't doing its job.

To relieve the pressure the engineer instructed his men to blast a gap in the by-wash wall. Nothing – the gunpowder was wet and failed to explode. Soon, a waterfall was crashing over the dam 'like a white sheet in the darkness', flooding into the fracture. I try to imagine his incredulous stare as a breach thirty yards wide appeared in the embankment, followed by the cacophony of total collapse. At that moment he knew it was 'all up.' The valley would soon be deluged with a biblical flood.

∾

In the low village, a city kicks back in paradise. On the benches by the cricket field day trippers simulate civil engineering: felling chocolate flake trunks at the base, chomping away at ice cream moraine, right down to the hard cornet.

By the road, an oldster on his bike – beige shorts, calf-length socks – blasts Chantilly Lace from a device in his rucksack – beige canvas, leather straps. Age warning, like a van's reverse alarm. Loose, like a long-necked goose. A beige shoe pushes down hard on a pedal, a sharp twist of the handlebars, a skid in the gravel and he's off. It's 1959 and he's fifteen again. 'Oh baby, that's what I like.'

Out in the middle, they're all out for a hundred and seventy – an athletic catch by the racing snake at extra cover. A wiry old roller heads out with his contraption of concrete and rusted metal. By the tennis court the lad recalls a friendly match when he was younger. Memories crystallise – crossing the narrow footbridge over the stream with Mum and the Matriarch. Everything the same, save for a fresh coat of white gloss paint on the handrails.

The path takes us by the river, up winding stone steps through the trees, then along a narrow gennel to the road at the top, by the wall of a different dam. It was here that the Sailor parked his light blue

Mk2 Escort, its black vinyl roof concealing bolt holes where they'd removed the police sign. Heading for the Bog beyond the reservoir, kitted out with binoculars, a compact Minolta and a shiny Velbon tripod in a leatherette case. Bird books and walking boots, a serviceable shirt and a Harris Tweed cap.

On the reservoir's north shore we follow the path through the woods, transported to a lakeside resort in sunnier climes, pestered by hyperventilating water company signs:

UNEVEN AND SLIPPERY SURFACE. RISK OF FALLING. DANGER DEEP WATER. BATHING PROHIBITED. HIGH RISK OF DROWNING.

And in case none of that worked:

WARNING: BLUE-GREEN ALGAE BLOOMS.

But the smiling mums in swimming costumes, splashing with their kids, and the paddle boarders out on the water seem to be surviving so far.

A friend spots us from a distance – somehow inevitable in this city of half a million – and hollers over. The sports bag on her shoulder contains a towel and a swimsuit – ready for an illicit dip. The game, she explains, is to dodge the water company lackey – a frustrated Chief Spoiler with no means of enforcement, just a yellow gilet. And she tells the story of one wild-swimming hero who has distilled the practice into performance art.

On the west side, the reservoir narrows and elongates – like a cat's tail about a hundred yards wide at the base. The swimmer loiters on the north shore until High Vis approaches, then sets off with a flawless front crawl. The company enforcer is duty bound to pursue him, but without his cossie it's a half-hour walk up to the tip of the tail and back down again. Our hero relaxes on the south shore until he nears, then launches off once more, back to his starting point. Presumably this carries on for hours. I imagine it all in the style of nineteen seventies visual comedy: fast-motion, Yakety Sax soundtrack, the chubby, breathless official sweating and mopping his brow. Chased by a pack of wild bathers in bikinis, abundant bosoms bouncing…

∾

The low village nestles in an improbably picturesque hollow, overseen by the gracious Norman church of its hilltop twin. Its vulnerable location, little more than a mile down the valley from the breached dam, isn't immediately obvious. But on 11th March 1864, the battering ram of water reached here after just three minutes.

Faced with the inadequacy of words to describe what he'd seen, the corn miller mobilised florid Victorian prose. The bowels of the earth were torn up, he wrote. Some unheard-of monster crunched up buildings between his jaws, filling the air with his wrathful hiss. It still wasn't enough.

Bridges, houses, smithies and the new Wesleyan School were swamped and shattered in seconds. Here, the first in a catalogue of deaths was recorded – a two-day-old baby snatched by a wave and swept away.

∾

We leave the cricket field behind us, passing the garage with a Mark 2 Jag rusting on the forecourt. Then we follow the tree-lined lane towards the third dam on our route – another of the Sailor's old haunts. Gaps in the foliage expose Kodak snaps of sails on the water. Sunlight and wavelets collide like camera flashes. Solo sailors lean out to level their Lasers, beating to windward, tacking to port then to starboard, twisting and ducking as booms swing across. In his younger years the Sailor would have been out there on a day like this. There's an old photo of him by the clubhouse, some time in the sixties, inspecting a wooden boat with a fellow enthusiast. In the background, a family alights from an Austin 8: father in a suit and tie, mother in a floral dress, the girls immaculate in starched white cotton and hair ribbons. Sunday out at the dam. There seems to have been a calmness in his expression when he was near the water. Contented. In his element.

In little bays below the path, bathers wet their feet and feel the sun on their skin. Mums swaddle shivering kids in giant towels. A group of ripped Balkan lads build a fire, their music carrying them home to bluer Adriatic waters. Two young women strip down to nipple barbells and cartoon tatts. A new world with a refreshing mood of live and let live.

Beyond the dam wall the road rises and the valley unfurls. Emerald meadows slope down to the deep wooded gully where, in 1864, the torrent built velocity, thrusting towards the city with devastating force. The hamlet that stood here was devoured: the bridge and the Barrel Inn, the labourers' cottages, the wire, paper and corn mills. Machinery ripped from anchors entered a deadly aggregate of tree trunks, stones and animal carcasses, driven along in a mighty liquid matrix. The settlement died that day, never to be rebuilt, but its name lives on in the reservoir, constructed after the flood.

The view from up here reminds us of the city's origins – in spokes of industry stretching out along river valleys. Far below us a postcard landscape of dray horses and dry-stone walls collides with a wreckage of redundant brick factories. Death risk for curious teenagers, leverage for housing developers pitching for planning permits. A side road leads us down there and we track the river for a while. Nature thrives but nothing's really natural – sluice gate gears and iron footbridges, footings of devastated rolling mills, water channelled between sheer, navvie-built walls. The flood left a wasteland in its wake. An opportunistic joint venture realised the valley's reconstruction – the creator in partnership with Victorian capital.

The path diverts around a fenced-off zone of dereliction, leading us up the wooded hillside, away from the river, through a miniature forest of nettle, bramble and pink campion. Descending again, we pass through a landscape scarred by spoil mounds and excavated hollows – traces of quarries and mines where ganister was extracted to feed the brickworks. Fossils were the foundation of everything here: petrified trees to fuel the city's fires, the remains of their nourishing soils to resist the heat. The factory fulfilled the transformation – washing, crushing and grading silica-rich stones, grinding them with water to a viscous clay, moulding the clay to be baked in kilns, forming firebricks to line the city's furnaces.

Emerging from the woods, passing a terrace of workers' cottages, we reach the site of the old factory where the Sailor worked in the sixties – demobbed from the navy, maintaining lorries that delivered bricks to the city's steelworks. I try to picture him here but fail to conjure his image from the cracked concrete and industrial decay. Only the sight of the works' bowling club, still in use and bearing the old company name, sparks a moment of connection.

From the bowling green, the footpath leads us over a bridge, through an island meadow, humming with sounds of spring, and back into the trees. Gradually the trail deteriorates – overwhelmed by brambles, collapsing into the river in places. Then it ends abruptly, encountering a vertical rock face.

A novice-level challenge, we think, a welcome frisson of risk on an otherwise undemanding outing. So we clamber to the top. But once there we've nowhere to go. To our right a sheer embankment rises above us, to our left a precipitous cliff descends to the river below.

This, it transpires, is to be our place of reckoning. The older man can think only of pressing on. He slips and almost falls, clutching on pathetically to a clump of wild garlic. Between gasps, he floats his brilliant plan: they'll climb the bank using tree roots as handholds, then – somehow – vault over the barbed wire fence at the summit. The lad takes a moment to engage his brain – someone has to – then comes back with a plan of his own.

'The best thing', he says, 'is to go back.'

Back. A simple and, it turns out, effective tactic, but one beyond the wits of the more experienced traveller.

I rationalise all this as evidence of a world-weary half-centurion's death drive, juxtaposed with the young man's indomitable will to survive. The reality is less dignified: a slapstick – albeit near fatal – encounter between neglected municipal infrastructure and a middle-aged idiot who shouldn't be allowed out. We retrace our steps, cross the bridge again and take the wheelchair-friendly path on the other side.

'Easy Going Trail', my companion reads out loud. 'Now there's a plan for life.'

At Little Matlock, the Friends of the Valley – pink gloves and sun hats, trowels and action trousers – are out in force, planting flowers against an impeccably patinated wall. A terrace of white, three storey cottages – stone lintels, sash windows – promises a life of rural perfection. Down in the hollow, the old hand-rolling mill keeps on rolling.

Here, where the valley flattens out to the north, a wider expanse succumbed to the flood's destructive force. In a terraced house by the river, a wealthy young forger drowned with his wife, their two young boys and their domestic servant – a girl of seventeen.

∾

With the hamlet behind us the path stretches ahead into the distance – dusty, dry and exposed, apparently never ending. The sun pesters us with malice, searing our necks, baking our hair. My companion flounders in the heat – red-faced and sweaty, wheezing like emphysema, firing missiles of snot and pollen from an aggravated nose. Then, our goal within reach, he drops his bombshell.

That's it, he says, flouncing. He's done. No more weird adventures. He's had his fill of grim history walks, the bloody ganister obsession, and now a near-death experience. But when I point out the bus stop by the road ahead of us, our portal back to the air-conditioned car at the top of the valley, he brightens up and quickens his step. It wasn't all that bad. He might come next time. If it's shorter. And less ridiculous. For now I'm off the hook. The team will ride again.

∾

It was important to reach our objective – the disaster's fulcrum. Falling short would have seemed disrespectful. At Malin Bridge the valley narrows to a bottleneck, traversed by the suburb's namesake where two rivers intersect. Today it's a peripheral place, favoured by sundry vendors of popular pleasures: chip shop, paintball outfit, sports bar, caravan megastore. In 1864 it was still a village, but expanding virally – industrialists jostling for prime riverside plots, immigrant workers crammed into rented, rickety huts. Some of the houses, including those of the wealthy, stretched out into the river on exposed promontories. All the pieces were in place for a catastrophe.

So when the flood hit, with massive, concentrated force, no one had a hope in hell. In the words of one observer, 'a bombardment with the newest artillery could hardly have proved so destructive'.

The Sailor's family had their roots around here: the father who fought in his Queen's imperial war, grandparents who might have borne witness, at least to the devastated aftermath. To me the story was unreal – a grainy daguerreotype or a school assembly play in period costume. But to him it was tangible trauma, resonating in living memory. That explained his fascination, and the well-thumbed book with the orange sleeve on the shelf beside his chair.

The flood followed river courses towards the city centre, inundating factories and the poor workers' houses clustered around them. At the Island the workhouse was overwhelmed, its inmates drowned behind bolted doors. Corpses, furniture and machinery were swept away and deposited in different towns, miles away downstream.

The city suffered terrible losses – two hundred and thirty eight deaths, six hundred houses destroyed or damaged, another five thousand flooded. While perhaps not the most notorious, this might have been the worst civilian disaster of the Victorian age.

At the inquest into the dam's collapse the jury noted failures of skill and diligence, but the Waterworks Company avoided blame. Its representatives introduced a counter-narrative – a landslip was responsible. The story gained some credence through repetition by gentlemen.

The company *did* accept liability, but then sought Parliament's permission to increase the water rate by twenty-five percent – enough to cover the cost of compensation. In this way, the flood's victims footed the bill.

The world changes on the surface but the underlying formations remain the same. By coincidence, in the week of writing this, the commercial water companies of our age have apologised, collectively, for dumping sewage in rivers and lakes. They'll invest billions, they say, to make up for their mistakes. There are no prizes for guessing who's going to pay.

This Is What a City Looks Like When Everything's Been Stolen

My vantage point was a gaudiesque perch at the top of Devonshire Green. A rare sunlit day in early November. A first outing for the winter coat. Taking a break from low productivity for an hour of me-time – to sit, watch, and generally do nothing at all.

The subject of my observations was a street cleaning operative, paused on the pavement by the pay and display car park. A giant of a man with a beard in proportion, towering over a metal cart with the tools of his trade arrayed on top. Primed for action.

His presence was welcome. The streets all around us were strewn with chip papers, pop cans and crisp packets, now blended with the current season's leaf fall into a muesli of urban misery, all on top of the tree fibres that still clogged the gutters from the previous autumn.

The obvious tactic would have been to select the stiff, broad brush from his arsenal, to trawl the pavement from east to west with a merciless dragnet. The application of overwhelming force. But his actions seemed irrational, inexplicable. The broom remained in its holster. Instead he picked a puny picker, like a withered orthopaedic arm, and used it to snatch a single chocolate wrapper from the summit of a mountain of leaves and litter.

This, I thought, was some kind of innovation: surgical, SWAT-team street sweeping, founded on superior, esoteric intelligence, homing in on high-value targets. And yet he displayed no signs of satisfaction. It might have been anomie or alienation. One way or another, this worker wasn't happy.

On my way to the bus stop, by the tradesmen's entrance to the theatre, I witnessed something similar. With a feeble, six-inch-wide scraper another forlorn sanitation technician was persecuting a single dandelion in the block paving. Taking a pen knife to a nuclear conflagration. The city, by now, had endless square miles of weed-riddled pavements. Why did this one warrant special attention? (And why no chemical warfare solution?)

Later, back in my home office, I mulled over the experience. Genuine grievance coincided with a new opportunity for work avoidance. I would call the Corporation, satisfying an urge to busybody that was only getting worse since I'd turned fifty.

The woman on the phone was suspicious, evasive. A troublemaker, asking too many questions. For my call to be forwarded, the full details of this voter and city taxpayer would need to be added to yet another database. Name, address, date of birth… It was as though I'd called the switchboard of the Security Service with a casual request for information about their top-secret, anti-terror operations.

I squeezed myself through an almost impossible gap to speak with some kind of customer service person. He was friendly, laid back.

"Was the Corporation enforcing its street cleaning contract properly?" I asked.

There was a team that had meetings with the outsourced service provider, he said. But he wouldn't call it 'enforcing the contract.' The ambience, he suggested, was more like a church coffee morning. Besides, they'd assessed the contract and termination was impossible. Legal costs.

No doubt the company knew this too. A vision of the meeting crystallised in my mind: the two parties seated around a leather-topped Town Hall table, sipping tea, exchanging pleasantries, while the representatives of a billion-turnover business politely crushed the Corporation officers' metaphorical balls.

Having clarified the sorry situation from his side, the Corporation man transferred me to the outsourcing company itself, ensconced – I was surprised to find – in the same office. It was my good fortune to be passed to someone who seemed fairly normal – transferred at some point from the local authority, naive in the dark arts of public relations.

I explained my concern and posed a simple question: did he think they were making a good job of cleaning the city's streets? His reply was considered and curiously formulated:

"I would say we're *doing* street cleaning."

"Yes… but are you doing a good job?"

"I'm not calling it a good job. We're doing *the* job."

(Everything recounted here was written down by me, at the time, as accurately as possible. I also understand the Corporation recorded the call for training and monitoring purposes. I like to imagine the incriminating tape locked up in a secure vault, deep in the bowels of the Town Hall.)

For a few minutes we reminisced fondly about how, back in the day – implicitly before his transfer, when the Corporation did the job itself – the city's streets had been so much tidier than they were now.

An unexpected call back the following day, from one of his superiors, cast light on what "doing *the job*" (rather than "*a good job*") actually meant. Once again, I was impressed by his honesty and, to begin with at least, his friendly demeanour. He explained that the company's obligation was to fulfil the performance requirements set out in the contract, which specified how frequently particular streets had to be visited.

I asked for clarification. Was he saying the targets related to showing up rather than clearing up?

"That's about the gist of it," he said.

There was, he added, a further complication. The city's parks and housing association estates were maintained by different outsourced contractors. Which explained the accumulations of litter at territorial boundaries:

"That's your fag packet."

"Not bloody likely, it's yours!"

Meanwhile the rats feasted and the city drowned in filth.

Towards the end of the call he lost his rag a bit (I admit I may have been a little robust myself). How dare I criticise the quality of the work delivered by his excellent team! The company valued them so much (he didn't add) that it paid them peanuts while reporting profits of almost a hundred million. (Why is it always a hundred million?) I wasn't criticising the workers, I said, I was criticising the business. But I think he knew that. The man in charge of our street lights was, you might say, gaslighting me.

Finally, he emphasised that the contract between the Corporation and his company was entirely transparent and available online. And there it was: a matrix setting out the service delivery output element, or some such waffle, and the performance requirement, with another column fully redacted in solid black blocks. Commercial in confidence. Completely transparent. Except where it wasn't.

Damn! With all this squabbling I'd forgotten to ask about the leaves. But they obviously weren't included in the contract. Perhaps the Corporation legal eagle responsible had drafted the relevant clause late on a Friday afternoon.

But the exercise had, at least, explained the odd behaviour and evident unhappiness of the operatives I'd seen in town. Contract fulfilment to the minimum required level prohibited them from doing a good job. Thus were they denied the possibility of satisfaction in their work.

Whatever was happening here, it wasn't street cleaning. It was something else entirely: a perversion of performance management, municipal services reinvented as performance art. And the thing performed was a conjurors trick, in which more of our money was taken for less than we had before.

Just one more example of what a city looks like when everything's been stolen.

A Different Animal

It's not unusual these days for citizens to look at this place and despair: the rubble-strewn gaps between buildings, endlessly awaiting development, the vape shops and vacant units, the library and art gallery's crumbling facade – symbols of municipal poverty. Other cities are better. Opportunity is elsewhere. That's why some of us leave and never look back: metropolitan big hitters, New World prospectors, antipodean escapees, disguising identities and diluting accents, embracing the condescension of adopted homes. The city's pitiful. An embarrassment.

If you're under fifty it's all you'll have known – the demolition balls swung before you even left school. Most of us are oblivious to what was lost. But High Street's smashed department stores and the old East End's industrial canyons told a different story. Once this was a massive place, where a young woman could stand, fixated before glistening window displays of designer dresses with capelets and boleros, imagining she was on the Champs-Élysées, and whose workers were cocksure, knowing their materials were building the modern world.

Destruction came in multiple waves, only one of which was the three-hundred-bomber raid that left the city in ruins on Friday 13th. Too much of what survived was sacrificed to the modernist gods: Cole's Corner and the Corn Exchange, countless theatres and picture palaces, aerated concrete replacing eternal gritstone, communities razed for high-rise towers and ring roads. Then the factories faltered before their final erasure in an act of imperial spite (compare it with how they rescued the banks). Prosperity turned to poverty. Vultures feasted on the city's carcass. Out-of-town speculators chewed up and regurgitated town planners, rebuilding East Hecla as a retail black hole to swallow the credit cards of redundant machinists.

In the centre, the jewellers, drapers, clothiers and purveyors of aspirant, ideal lifestyles faltered. Charity shops and Christmas pop-ups took their places. Offshore entities demolished vacant blocks, creating eyesores to blackmail a shrivelled municipality. A beaten population stood by and watched, the fight knocked out of them, waiting for saviours.

Those who came were time-clock consultants from a distant continent – prophets in a different country. Ignorant of history, oblivious to context and idiosyncrasy, they noted that this place lacked 'city-ness' – an absence of mass lurking in the gaps left by Messerschmitts, monetarists, asset strippers and warriors of competing classes. The locus of the problem, they said, was the middle – 'the hole in the donut'. They pulled out their blueprint for the model metropolis with its centralised cerebrum – a single seat of knowledge and power positioned inside the ring road.

They were right about the hole, but wrong about the donut. Because this city isn't concentric, it's stellate.

The city's intelligence and potency stretch out along narrow valleys radiating from the centre – erstwhile cradles of water-driven industry, each hosting its own, ultra-local culture, identity and tribal community. Variously anti-establishment, liberal or traditional, their origins are native, national/continental, or Empire-immigrant, their conditions affluent, impoverished, or precariously in the middle. Their uniforms are football shirts and industrial workwear, fleeces and hiking boots, thobes and hijabs, or wax jackets and managers' suits. Denominated by unique geo-numerical codes, each exists in semi-isolation from the others, divided by wooded hills and inadequate communications.

With their mammalian mindset, the visiting experts searched for sophistication at the centre, only to find arrested development. Their subject, they concluded, was a witless ungulate.

But this city's different. Because this city's a cephalopod.

Like the octopus, with decentralised brains in each of its semi-autonomous arms, the city's functions and capabilities are distributed. Its appendages operate independently. The central brain, hosting only a minority of neurons, exerts limited control.

The city's dispersed micro-minds are its extended urban villages, its richness and vitality contained in their working men's clubs and rock climbers' pubs, shisha lounges and grand mosques, pork sandwich or fishing tackle shops, lock-up garages and racing pigeon lofts. These are the settings for autonomous, disobedient lives. The centre exerts control but tentatively, with limited authority. When the parking enforcers finally arrived in our forgotten hollow, flashing their tickets with ill-concealed satisfaction, they had all the legitimacy of Carabinieri in a remote Sicilian village:

"You can't do that!"

"Yes, I can. You're parked on a double yeller."

"You can't. I've been parking on these double yellers for twenty years!"

In the fortunate, richer suburbs, the absence of police reinforces the sense of independence, not to mention safety.

The fact is that most of us, most of the time, don't really live in the city, immersing ourselves in it. We just cross it on valley roads, following river courses from suburban homes to the central hole or a remote retail park. Through our car windows we disregard scenes blurred by familiarity, knowing little of the complex, linear worlds we're passing through.

And so we fail to see the mollusc's distinctive genius.

Visitors, forgivably, do the same – underwhelmed town-centre wanderers searching in vain for a better retail or cultural offer. (The city's wonders are walkable, but it takes a day and a decent pair of shoes.)

We can stretch our analogy to its limits: octopuses have large optic lobes – watching is central to their lifestyle. Like this place they're fragmented and fascinating, mischievous and clever (in an unusual way), ugly and beautiful, with strange body plans and, perhaps, multiple selves. (There's no blue blood here, though, unless we count the Duke's.)

So leave this place, of course you will – there's a bigger, richer world out there. And if you're unimpressed, that's fine, it's up to you. But consider this: it could be worth taking another look. Because it might just be that this city's a very different animal from the one you thought you knew.

The River – Part Seven

Regeneration. Cast concrete steers the river between unlet offices and flats the size of Nordic prison cells, near the gym where small print sucks you in and estate agents gather in a greasy steam room. Then it's gone, devoured by the thuggish ring road that slices the city in two.

In the car park of a city centre subprime warehouse, the culvert roof has caved in. Smart bomb aesthetics. A craggy entrance to Hades. Beyond Mary Street the river appears, then vanishes on repeat, hidden behind keystoned arches, funnelled between factories repurposed for media industries. Diminished, disoriented, integrity eroded – a serial abuse victim.

The Duke

It may not have escaped the reader's attention that a villain of this parish pantomime is a character identified only as the Duke – a time-lord incarnate across centuries, appearing in multiple physical forms, not unlike Beelzebub himself.

His immense wealth, said to exceed a hundred million (why is it always a hundred million?), has its origins in a fortuitous gift from a 14th-century king. Since then, apart from occasional issues with the male issue, persecution for popery, incarceration in the Tower and execution by decapitation, it's been a walk in the eponymous park.

It was the Duke's good fortune that a global centre of industry happened to grow on one of his manorial estates. By the late Victorian age his landholdings here yielded enough in one year to keep a family in luxury for generations – from rents, mineral rights and the markets (which, by another stroke of luck, were his too – it's all right when you're Lord of the Manor).

All of which explains why, wherever we turn in this city, the Duke taunts us with his esoteric titles and ubiquitous wealth, demanding implicit tribute in our streets, schools, parks and pubs, bounding onto the stage of our provincial playhouse with another identity and its own absurd costumery – soldier, Duke, Baron or Earl: the ceremonial red tunic of a Territorial Army colonel (stepping up when the King calls for cannon fodder), the crimson velvet, miniver and ermine of a constitutionally entitled aristocratic weasel, the gold-braided tailcoat and baton of a better class of royal party organiser (this one specialising in kingly accessions and state funerals – don't search here for paper hats and balloons.) The double-breasted suit of the cold-eyed rentier.

The Duke doesn't live around here of course (it could be the litter or land-bank dereliction that puts him off). He's said to make occasional trips up from the family seat to scrutinise the rent collection, evaluate the extraction, perhaps also to assert his primacy in the parallel, albeit opaque, hierarchy that really counts when the shit hits the fan – from the grovelling local establishment through the King's representative in the county to the monarch and chief of the (tooled-up) armed forces himself. Let democracy deal with the bins and potholes but never, ever let go.

It was reported recently that a local politician, in a superb display of old-school tubthumping, excoriated the Duke for squeezing the maximum price from a parcel of land required by the Corporation for affordable housing. Same story, different century. In his defence, the Duke explained that life's not so easy – he needed the cash. And it's a fair point when you've at least one castle to run.

At which point I check myself. All this fault-finding, but what's my position here? An essential theme of this piece is the intrinsic value of idleness. And, as has been noted, the circles of self-rule and work ethic only partially intersect in our Venn diagram.

Which compels me to conclude that the Duke may, in fact, be one of us. After all, he's been hanging around here long enough.

Time Travellers

In the living room I find the boy sprawled on the sofa in the shape of a newly discovered deep-sea life form, doom-scrolling digital renderings of old nitrate and acetate film reels, casting them to the TV from his cornucopia of videos (and everything else besides). Their titles catch my attention. I hadn't expected this of him, I thought it was just me:

The Old City, A City Through Time, The Secret City, A City for People, International City, The City in the '60s, A City on the Move, 1970s Demolition. And so it goes on…

Because it's the way these things work, a moment of curiosity has released a deluge of related material, leading to deep immersion in a warm, therapeutic bath of Panglossian retrospectives, cleansing everything from brutalist underpasses to Corporation sink estates, eventually convincing him that his new-found knowledge of obscure civic history was acquired through the exercise of his own free will.

But I know what's happening here, and the algorithm isn't entirely to blame.

At last he stops all his flicking and clicking. Like that magical moment in the cinema we fall silent as opening credits roll – hooked by mournful violins and lonely, tinkling piano notes that drip like liquid gold (or the sweet tears of an incurable nostalgist).

A turn-of-the-century tram ride draws us in, leading us along narrowing tracks down Fargate, High Street, Haymarket and Waingate towards an impossible vanishing point, beckoned by a lucid conductor who stares into the camera lens and our souls across the ages, curious to look into the eyes of the living. Finally he turns away, crushed by disappointment.

Pavements throng with porters, shoppers, burghers, office and industrial workers – ladies in flowing skirts and lace-embellished blouses, gentlemen in frock coats with umbrellas folded, clerks in suits and round collars, draymen in waistcoats with shirt sleeves rolled. All waiting, watching, rushing or peering into shops under signs peddling mint rock, drugs, or linen gloss soap, tents and marquees – for hire or sale, oilskins and waterproofs. The frenetic commercial energy of the Belle Époque and an Empire on a roll.

In the road, eclectic vehicles weave between gas lamps and catenary poles: tramcars moved by mysterious electrical currents, carriages and omnibuses powered by a thriving equine population – awaiting annihilation, haulage drays groaning beneath piles of boxes or agricultural produce. Careless street wanderers skip, stagger or somnambulate in fractional gaps between deadly wheels – a girl alone in an open-back pinafore, a little boy lost and confused, a smart young couple thrashing a souped-up perambulator.

On the slope of Commercial Street a white blouse back frames an exquisite ponytail, resolutely life-affirming in a crowd of grayscale corpses. Skirt pleats ripple as her hips sway – striding concisely to an important diary appointment. Beauty and youth in their immutable, universal forms, transcending justification.

She might have been obscured for a second by a passing tramcar, only to reappear as the blue bulk of its modern iteration proceeds towards Hyde Park, now, in this very moment, captured in a window arch of the United Gas Light Company, suit trousers pinched at the waist by the same leather belt, her white shirt illuminating the same immaculate hairstyle. A time-travelling Immortal untethered from the ages.

The film finishes with a 'Then and Now' juxtaposition: Waingate before and after the twentieth century's destruction and reconstruction – from filigree window frames to a collapsing Old Town Hall, the stained concrete cliff of the magistrates court, skint shoppers waiting in the rain at a vandalised bus stop.

With the closing credits the boy presents his conclusion:

'Everything was just better then, wasn't it?'

'Everything?'

'Yeah. Look at their clothes and all the shops and the crowds of people in town. That's what a city should look like.'

I consider the things we've seen for a moment: palpable, if harshly uneven, prosperity, abundant public transport powered by electricity (unpolluting at the point of use), streets with space for pedestrians and cyclists (unprompted by Corporation active travel campaigns), a thriving commercial centre (walkable in fifteen minutes from pre-demolition inner suburbs).

The city in those days was a productive machine, its component parts – not all jewels but every one essential – integrated like clockwork, directed towards an output of incontrovertible value: the material from which modernity and progress were formed. Lubricated by something intangible but discernible in expressions, the clothes people wore and the ways they walked: *belief* – in their city, their Empire, their emancipation or their trade union, in progress itself – something people today seem to be mourning, desperate to rediscover.

What's our purpose now? In this age of disintegration, when the movement's mainspring and gears have been stripped out and cashed in, leaving behind redundant pieces seeking solace in fast-food gimmicks and limitless, degenerate consumption. The wheel has turned and we're back where we were – in an unforgiving age of winners and losers, but this time without the finery, power or accomplishment.

But because my early life and indoctrination coincided with the Age of Progress, part of me feels obliged to counter with the argument that things today must, inevitably, be better.

'Didn't you see that pauper on Pinstone Street?' I posit. 'And who cared about their health? Besides, they had no idea a global catastrophe was just around the corner.'

The boy smiles at me gently, with love and pity, detecting well-intentioned insincerity, acknowledging our deeper connection. Because he sees the same things I see – machinery broken, hands disconnected. We suffer from the same illness. Like tuberculosis it thrives among those who live in unhealthy proximity. Four adults in a three-bedroom semi, for example.

Happy? Not Happy.

Nothing around here seems to work any more. At first, for a while, there was a reason, or at least an explanation, perhaps just a credible excuse. Now it's just the way things are – the New Normal.

I called the doctor with a minor illness that would, in my childhood, have been diagnosed as a 'poorly finger.' The receptionist – that ruthless gatekeeper – did everything possible to put me off. The doctor could speak to me in five weeks, she said, presumably via the internet.

To state the obvious, by then my condition would either have cured by itself or else all my limbs would have been removed in emergency surgery for sepsis. In the end I resorted to the usual cocktail of healing creams and ointments passed down from the Matriarch and, God knows which, other wise women before her, all containing active ingredients derived from marigolds or the bees – calendula, propolis, royal jelly.

It's just how we do things these days, in this post-enlightened age of cyclical instead of linear progression, in which, once again, trust is placed in balms and supernatural fate over inaccessible, scientific medicine.

A month later, laid low with a mild fever and a sore middle digit, I concluded that my medieval remedies weren't working. So I called the practice again, engaging with the same, snarling rottweiler at perimeter security. The doctor could see me in five weeks, she said, without much interest, although it might be by text. That's what I was told before, I said. It was too long to wait.

Later that day – at last – the doctor called me.

'I understand this is an *emergency,*' she said, accusingly.

'I didn't say…' I started to protest. But what's the point? Sometimes you just can't win.

I related the experience to my old mate, who shook his head in disappointment at my naivety. You need to *write* to the doctor, he said, with a fountain pen and bottled ink on your best watermarked stationery. Put 'esquire' at the end of his name – it'll make him feel special. And include another envelope, with your address and a first-class stamp on it, and a blank sheet of the same classy paper.

He'd recently corresponded with his own GP in exactly this way, starting his letter like this:

Dear Doctor C____

I trust you and your family are in good health. I'm writing to let you know that I'm suffering from a problem that, according to my medical encyclopedia, seems to be the gallbladder…'

The reply came quickly, by first class post (of course).

Dear Mr B____

My family and I are very well, thank you. Please call me straight away on my personal mobile…

~

At the bus stop, I've been waiting for twenty-five minutes. They used to come along every ten. I chat with the old lady who's standing there with me, holding a supermarket bag over her head to protect her hairdo from the rain.

'Oh well,' I say, looking down at the unusually smooth, black asphalt, 'at least they've finally resurfaced the pavement.'

'They have,' she replies, wearily. 'It's just a shame they demolished the bus shelter when they did it.'

~

Outside our house my wife was involved, you might say, in a minor collision. The neighbours had a visitor from a different city – one further south with flatter topography. He parked the car on our road in his habitual way – out of gear with the handbrake only lightly engaged. During the night it rolled down the hill, colliding with my wife's car and damaging its back end. She called the insurance company to explain and lodge a claim.

'So, it was a collision? Were either of the cars stationary at the time or were they both being driven?'

'No. Neither of the cars had anyone in them.'

Silence.

'Were you driving your car at the time?'

'No, I've just said, both of the cars were empty'.

Silence.

'Do you have the details of the person who was driving the other vehicle?'

'I've just said…' But once again it was futile. The car boot still leaks to this day.

∾

Finding a tradesman is more or less impossible. But in the end, we got lucky, a floor fitter showed some interest. So we booked a date.

Just before the work was due to begin, he called us, offering his apologies. He couldn't make it, he said. A bereavement in the family. What with the funeral and all, could we reschedule for a fortnight hence?

Two weeks later he cancelled again. There'd been a death in the family, he said, apparently forgetting to shuffle his excuses. In the end I was glad he didn't show up. Knowing this man was clearly dangerous.

∾

In the discount store with the cheap toiletries there's a sign on the wall with two faces and corresponding buttons: green, with a smile, and red, with a frown. We're invited to give our feedback – Happy? Not Happy? – to help them improve their service (or maybe just to persecute the teenagers on the tills).

A kid's feeling good because his mum, satisfied with the low prices, has bought him more multi-packs of sweets than he could ever have dreamed of. So he slams away repeatedly at Happy in the familiar manner of the certified hyperactive. He hammers it with his fist at least twenty times but nothing happens. It just doesn't work. Eventually, less Happy than he was before, he smashes Not Happy, just the once. Immediately it lights up.

No longer interested, not giving a toss, he drags his chaotic limbs out of the shop.

Heimat

If it stood on its own, the semi would be perfectly defensible – poised on an escarpment high above the city, just down from the playing field once requisitioned for a hilltop air defence battery.

We moved in the day the city flooded, styled as shipwreck victims. The road, with its absurd gradient, was running like rapids, overwhelming culverts down in the valley. (The water height that day is marked on the pub wall at Alma Street. A second white line, higher up, shows the level in 1864, after the dam collapsed.)

But the house remained above the fray – invincible, its front door six feet from the ground because the land falls away, accessed by perilous steps with a grab rail for traumatised pensioners. Which makes the elevation unusually high – a sheer cliff of furnace-blackened bricks, bastion against winter north winds. (Most of the year, the sky – a roll of calico dabbed with lugubrious clouds – scrolls from west to east, while Zephyrus perches on the proscenium arch, cranking his handle, dangling his feet).

From the front bedroom bay on a clear day you can play I spy with city landmarks: the TV transmitter on Tapton Hill – ready to launch from its spaceframe tower, spoiled earth at Parkwood Springs, the bulk processing plant for births and inevitably deaths, but mostly repair and maintenance, the spire of the church next door – provider of associated services. And visible through a latticework of twigs and telegraph cables: the penthouse of a Netherthorpe tower block, the university's red-brick battlements – defending rankings and reputations, the elevated motorway's bold double underline, the retail siren and her sexier Scandinavian cousin.

The boy's room is across the landing – repainted now in a deeper, adult shade of blue. But the view from the window endures: the water tower rising at the eastern horizon – charcoal scratched on a pastel hue, cherry branches melted by sunlight – a lawn striped with shadows, muscular gangs of goldfinch mods and magpie rockers – eyeballed by a crow with a doorman's demeanour and shiny black jacket. White vapour rising from a boiler vent – did someone just make a decision?

At the end of the garden you can stand on the grassy mound where the Anderson's bricks and iron roof are buried – for a different perspective: cemetery gatehouse, cholera monument, model valley estate with crumbling maisonettes, fleeting white tips of windmill blades above the hill's brow – advancing giants waving their arms.

And if you listen carefully, you can dismantle the ambient hum: garden geese squabbling – living the Good Life, sparrow spouses flapping – privet hedge nesting, delighted children's voices – school break-time, turbofans ascending – the thirteen-ten from Ringway. The train horn that slices through it all – a wistful exhalation, someone leaving home.

And I can look down on the corner patio and rewind my cerebral video: two boys in a cardboard box car with invisible kids in the back, smashing castles in the sandpit, frying plastic eggs on a toy stove in the shed we nearly burned down on bonfire night.

A slender mountain ash stands on that mound, in memory of the old lad who used to live here. He fought his way through Normandy in a Churchill tank, then settled into a job at the Atlas Works. At weekends, with his pal from next door, they built their garages and garden paths of concrete with pebble aggregate.

The day we locked ourselves out, the locksmith spotted the combination box on the wall by the door.

'Was she an old lady from the war? Try 1945. If not, 1944.'

He was right second time.

In the house I try to keep the old things intact – lengths of string connecting us to the past: the stained-glass window with the builder's family crest – a Deco knight in radiant blue and purple segments; the brown, brittle Bakelite door handles upstairs; the thirties stencils on the living room wall, safe behind temporary wallpaper. The carpenter's newspaper, dated 1960, that I put back under the lifted floorboard, the hand-fashioned cupboard in the cellar where the old lad kept his tins, the Matriarch's clock in the attic, wrapped in a shiny sheet, its broken pendulum laid on top.

It's a feeling that builds the more you contemplate it – assimilation with a setting and its unending vibrations: sounds, images and sensations, ghosts and memories like photographic negatives superimposed on the material city. A notion of spatial and temporal integration. A fantasy of rootedness. Someone, somewhere should find a word for it.

Velocity

The tide was already turning. People were already buying their clobber on the internet. Then the global pandemic struck. So when lockdown was lifted and masks were discarded, the city centre's last chain department stores kept their doors shut. A tired old couple unable to muster the strength to stagger on.

The locus of investment shifted. None of those online shoppers had a clue whether their trousers would fit properly. So they bought three pairs and sent two or sometimes all of them back. Then the smart money was in 'reverse logistics' – fulfilled in windowless reprocessing shacks out by the motorway.

But then, just as quickly, everyone decided that was all a bit of a drag. They were tired of picking up parcels from sullen neighbours, digital eye strain, never having reason to leave the house. The intangible retailers stumbled into insolvency, from the costs of shipping, handling, administering, inventorising and dispatching once again – three pairs of slacks for another vacillating consumer who only needed one (and probably planned to send *them* back the day after the wedding).

In the city centre there's continuous revolution. Three years ago department stores were the go-to places for jeans and chinos, doubling up as gilt-edged anchors for the latest regeneration scheme. Two years ago it was a full-length mirror on the landing, a freepost return bag and a sticker with a barcode. Last year, the trend spotters declared, in-person shopping was back. But this time the punters demanded more than a soulless transaction. It had to be boutique, with personal service, fresh coffee, ambience and mood music.

But even as the new, bijou shop units await their unchained occupants, the focus shifts again. Who wants to buy *stuff* anyway? Where do you even put it when your flat, in its rental-only block, is smaller than a Scandinavian punishment cell? Buying things is so twentieth century when your life's in the streets and you've everything you need in your hand-held cornucopia.

But being poorer than your parents – with your dreams of affluence bogged down in zero-hour jobs and student loans – does tell you one thing: live in the moment. Who needs soft furnishings and an outfit for every occasion? Experiences are everything. What you really need, in between festivals and weekends in bucket-list destinations, is an almost limitless selection of street food.

With a handbrake turn, the city centre takes another new direction – hastily reconceived as a venue for frenetic dining and drinks consumption, reverberating with live lounge music and laid-back conversation.

Within a short walk of your can't-swing-the-cat apartment, you can travel the gastronomic globe, from Thailand to Pakistan, Palestine, Eritrea and Vietnam, in an endless adventure of spicy marinades and sauces thickened with xanthan. In this sweet and sour life you'll never need to cook again, in your Lilliputian, ill-fitted kitchen.

But today the formula seems to be failing, at least in the gazebos that form a temporary, culinary bazaar around the Town Hall. Stand-up diners are thin on the ground. They've all been enticed to the giant new food hall with yet another anarcho-syndicalist identity. (If there were half as many communists here as the names of street food outlets imply, the place would be crawling with Security Service operatives).

For once, though, I'll take my hat off to the Corporation. The city centre's latest remake is thoughtfully done. There are signs of life in the hole in the donut. In the end, via a perilous, winding path, we dodged the misery of a massive indoor shopping centre, with foetid, conditioned air and gents-toilet floor tiles.

The thought has crossed my mind: if it's as transformational as the sales pitch suggests, this latest round of renewal could scupper my writing project – premised as it is on irreversible economic decline. But, really, I'm not too worried. I'm reminded of those before and after adverts you see, through clouds of particulates, on the backs of city buses – the once-chubby lad in the wake of his miracle diet, holding his enormous waistband out in front of him.

That man – too skinny to fill his joggers – is the city's post-industrial economy. Even the most inspired reinvention can't overcome the fundamental problem. You can build new shop space and the next generation of plucky entrepreneurs will have a go. But how can it work when the pie isn't growing and everyone's out, skint-shopping on shabby retail parks?

Every new, disruptive enterprise consumes an established predecessor. As one venture launches, another inevitably expires. How can anything survive in a world spinning this quickly, with ever-increasing velocity and ever-reducing friction? Where every new dawn arrives sooner than expected, turning yesterday's novelties into obsolete relics.

The city can't keep up. Unsanctioned demolition outpaces construction. Pedestrian precincts slide into disrepair then get ripped up for radical replacement – soon to be neglected and broken in turn. Perilous, unpredictable traps lie in wait for optimists – set by poverty, technology, pestilence or lightning-fast fashion. No one wants to part with their money – they've already met the affable robot whose job it is to make them redundant. Here at the periphery, recovery's always, almost within our grasp. But it wasn't before and it won't be this time either, because there's always too little to go round.

I'm all in favour of pitta bread and circuses, washed down with a can of hoppy pale ale, and the relaxed vibe sits well with the city's essential informality. But my heart's with the extended family we passed earlier in the day, sprawled on a tartan rug in the late spring rain, across the road from the Catholic cemetery, eating sarnies out of cling film on the riviera of an empty, azure-painted paddling pool. Lethargic musings on green shield bugs and wasps in egg fillings, just for the romance of it. Silent affection filling spaces unoccupied by extractive distractions. The soul of this city resides in things that will never make anyone any money. Which is a good thing, under the circumstances.

The River – Part Eight

Things look up at the newly built micropark – a semicircle sliced from a car park, turfed and terraced for open-air theatre in a planner's erotic dreams. The stage set: the eternal river, viscous with meaning, the wall behind gentrified with council-sanctioned graffiti, defaced with a rebel's tag in vulgar technicolour: TELL DA TRUTH.

Between the City Archive and the arts collective the river descends into the earth, where tributaries merge beneath station platforms. Leaving the city behind, their powerful progeny winds through coal and railway towns, valleys and flatlands, to the place where the Sailor sailed the Kan-Tiki – that fantastical contrivance of ropes, planks and oil cans.

Searching for the City's Soul

So this is a city with a soul. But where should we go in search of it?

The dead centre's a decent place to start, where Vulcan strikes a naked pose with his arrows, hammer and anvil – high above his furnaces and forges; friezes of blacksmiths, grinders and suited merchants; revellers stumbling in stilettos through the after-image of a fountain; the spiceman spilling lager on his gold, ladies' sandals.

Or it could be down the hill from there, on the ground floor of the city centre's last surviving department store, reliant now on a single, indomitable customer segment – menopausal and mature – perusing floral dresses while husbands linger in flat caps and anoraks, swaying titanium hips to a Muzak soundtrack that may or may not be incongruous: *It's getting hot in here, let's take off all our clothes.*

It sounds unlikely but you can feel it in the new development of steel and glass offices, between shallow water features and public art pieces, where they've lifted a brand-new section of granite paving then filled the hole with crumbly black tarmac. A temporary repair, reassuring in its permanence. The imperfect city rising up from below, reasserting its dominance.

There's potential too in that crack in the Central Library lobby floor – a line leading back to Fitzalan Square, the bomb that fell on the Marples Hotel and the young woman who passed by there in the morning – heading to work at the GPO.

I suppose it lingers like Woodbine smoke inside the walls of the old clubhouse – carrying lost voices of dancers, drinkers, band members and old-time stand ups, its current mood described in shade or sunlight in the recess over the front door.

There was a sighting not far from there, in the convenience store on the Pond at the top of Hallowmoor, late 2005, a wired Asian kid with a beginner's beard, drumming the latest rhythm on the blue screen of a lottery machine. A sign that read: 'It is illegal to sell tobacco products…'

You know it's with you on the moors up at Redmires where all the stories intersect, seeping into dams and flowing down to the city through iron pipes and the old, open conduit. And it lives in the rivers that grow from springs and streams on the high ground, following our life courses along the valleys, convening in subterranean caverns, continuing in unity towards the great estuary.

When I stood in Hecla's shadow on the cliff below the cemetery, I was sure I could hear it speaking to me.

About the Author

Nick Smillie was conceived on 14th February 1972, during the miners' strike and power cuts that marked the end of the post-war party. There was, he understands, not much else to do.

He grew up on 'Europe's largest private housing estate' at the disputed border of the Midlands and the northern city of his birth, which later became his home. After studying social anthropology he pursued a career in economic development and place marketing – telling stories about cities. But the stories they choose to tell aren't always the ones that make them fascinating.

Acknowledgements

Thanks to everyone who supported me in this endeavour: Rafa – my fellow traveller and sound-of-mind supervisor, Aurora – city walker and good-living guru, Alex – for always looking upwards, Mum – always unconditional, Dad – for the sound advice, Nev – for the chats, laughs and insights, Benji – for one or two choice phrases, Father Walsh – for welcoming a stranger and sharing time, Rob and Professor Matt – for helpful reviews along the way, Adam, Amanda and Carol – for the cover artwork, numerous city historians, writers and urban explorers – for a wealth of sources and stories, and Steve and 1889 Books – for taking this on and a collaboration that has been a real pleasure.

www.ingramcontent.com/pod-product-compliance
Lightning Source LLC
Chambersburg PA
CBHW040534170726
48295CB00012B/462

* 9 7 8 1 9 1 5 0 4 5 4 6 1 *